Make Independent

Computer
Games

Chapters

Who is this book for?	1
What will you learn	4
Ideas	5
Game concepts	8
The BIG questions	16
Psychology	22
Thinking differently	30
Interactive devices	42
The formula	67
Make your own "fruit slice" game	77
Make your own maze generator	93
Artificial Intelligence – A.I.	107
You're not finished	127
Test, test and test some more	131
The 'unknown' factor	133
Don't let reviews grind you down	136
Recap	144

About the author

Neil King is a software engineer who has been making computer games since the 1980s from the age of 10. More recently he has built himself a strong reputation in the I.T. industry for creativity and technical problem solving. Neil has developed cloud-based and stand-alone applications for multiple sectors including education, automotive, child safety, medical and gaming, and has had two number 1 best-selling apps in the App Store. His 20 years of experience in Further Education has enabled him to explain complex, technical instructions in an easy-to-understand way.

This book is dedicated to all of Neil's family and friends who have helped him along the way, particularly his daughter Abi who is both his biggest supporter and his inspiration.

Content & illustrations ©Neil King, 2023
ISBN: 9798867238681 – First Edition Paperback

Who is this book for?

This book is for anyone interested in learning how to create video games, from beginners to those already in the business. It is mainly aimed at the hobbyist or independent game maker, i.e. someone who wants to make popular games using their own time and resources. Some of it will certainly be appropriate for any game creator and even seasoned professionals will hopefully find it gives them food for thought. It's often useful to go over the basics from time to time so we don't lose sight of what's important.

You don't need to have any game making or programming experience to benefit from this book, but if you have done some coding or even simple game making in the past - great!

This book won't teach you how to code, although it does contain some "pseudo code" that you can easily convert to a language of your choice. Pseudo code is a simplified language which is used when designing software or programming routines. It is useful to jot down how something will work quickly or in generic terms without having to write perfect syntax. There are many programming languages, libraries and platforms that you can develop for so I don't want to focus on just one. Instead, you should get a much more rounded and useful knowledge base that will be of benefit to all languages and platforms. With an ever changing suite of development tools, this will help you to build games both now and in the future.

You should be able to use what you learn here no matter what device your game will run on or what programming language you choose for your game. As you progress it will get slightly more technical and more in-depth, so stick with it. The bite-sized chapters should be ideal to look back on during your game development journey and after you have finished, to double check you have asked yourself the right questions. There are also some useful explanations and examples to show you how things are or can be done.

There are some benefits of not working at a large games production company. When you are working for yourself or in a small team you have a lot more freedom to change things and drift away from a design plan.

If you are doing it as a hobby and aren't reliant on your games to make a living you can have a lot more fun with putting them together, remaking and tweaking them until YOU are happy. There is nothing to stop you approaching the big publishers if you make something special, or release it on your own and keep all of the glory and profits!

 Of course, you may not be able to afford the best tools but there are plenty of free, open source solutions which will only cost you the time it takes to learn how to use them.

Happy game making!

What will you learn?

That is the perfect question to ask when reading any text book. The table of contents shows the subject areas we will cover, but here is a concise bullet list of the things you should take away once you have finished.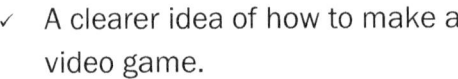

- ✓ A clearer idea of how to make a video game.
- ✓ Important things to research when designing your games.
- ✓ Some of the pitfalls to avoid when making a game.
- ✓ What makes a good game.
- ✓ An idea of the mind-set you need to make your game work the way YOU want it to.

There are a few things this book asks of you:

- ✓ A passion for computer games.
- ✓ A desire to make your own games.
- ✓ No previous game making skills are required.

Ideas

All game players think they have great ideas for games. The sad truth is that the vast majority of ideas actually won't or can't make a good game. That doesn't mean you shouldn't keep coming up with them and writing them down. Coming up with ideas can be the most difficult part of game making for some developers.

A tip for you:
Keep a log of ideas you have as you never know... piecing together several small parts from several ideas could make something really special.

An idea alone does not make a game, just like a story alone does not make a game. A story can be a large part of it but a story by itself has no interaction. A game must involve the player, drawing them in, giving them choices or testing their skill.

There are many games which don't have stories at all, such as most puzzle games or retro arcade games. I am sure everyone has played games which feel like the story has been tacked on afterwards without being necessary, but a game MUST have some form of interaction.

An idea must be turned into a game and may change significantly during the process for many reasons.

Perhaps it is too 'narrow', much like a traditional story and won't give the player enough freedom to make it enjoyable or feel they have any control.

Or maybe it is too 'vague' so the player won't know what to do, where to go, leading to frustration if their path is unclear. This can be particularly bad if it happens near the start of the game.

It can be a tricky balancing act to give the player enough choice and freedom without creating an overly-complex game where they struggle to know what to do. This is where tutorial levels can be useful to get the player to learn key functionality in a simpler "sandbox" area. It is perfect for players to learn basic controls, find out what they are looking for, perhaps defeat some very low-level enemies or puzzles, and collect some items or points.

Some games slowly introduce features which the player learns over time. When this is done well, the player may not even notice all of the skills they have developed as they are trickle-fed to them. A great example of this is "Horizon Zero Dawn" on the Playstation 4. Strategy or role-playing-games (RPGs) especially can end up having very complicated control systems so hand-holding players through the basics is a great way to introduce them to the game.

Sometimes game ideas just aren't feasible whether down to current technology or an unrealistic scope. For example, imagine a game where you can travel to any point in time, anywhere in the world and meet anyone throughout history. This sounds fantastic but would be completely unrealistic and impossible to create... at least for now. Remember though, what we thought was impossible 15 years ago are common in games now.

Game concepts

When you have decided to make a game, there are three main categories it could fall into:

 • A remake

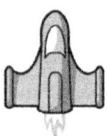 • A new game in an existing genre

 • A completely new type of game

It isn't always as easy as it sounds to pigeon-hole a game but 1 of these 3 categories should fit any game you can think of. There are occasions when a game may start out in one category while being developed and then move into another as new ideas and features are implemented. An example could be something that starts out as a remake before taking on a life of its own and becoming a new game in the same genre as the original. In fact, this is a great way to get started with your own games.

A remake

'Remakes' usually try and stay true to a previous game in terms of gameplay and story but may have improved graphics etc. to bring it up to date. Game 'clones' also fall into this category.

People often create 'remakes' of games they love, have fond memories of from years gone by, or sometimes because old games won't run on current devices. It could be that a game isn't available anymore so the only way to play it again is to remake it yourself.

The 'retro remake' market is much bigger than most people think, and mostly made by hobbyists like you!

The GOOD:

- ✓ It can be a great hobby project and certainly a good way to flex your game building skills.

- ✓ If you loved it, many other people probably did too.

- ✓ Development can be quicker as you can copy the game mechanics, level design etc.

The BAD:

- It may only ever be classed as a 'fan game' and not a game in its own right.

- You may never be able to make money from it due to copyright issues or simply because of the unoriginal concept. **WARNING:** Copyright can be an issue even if you don't make money from your game.

- It will always be compared to the original, so it needs to be able to stand up against it which can be tricky if the original was created by a big software house.

Examples of remakes include: Prince of Persia Classic, The Great Giana Sisters, and the millions of Flappy Bird clones.

A new game in an existing genre

There are many, many different genres of game which already exist such as first-person-shooters, racing, platform, point-and-click adventure, role-playing games, sliding puzzle games etc. To make a successful game in an existing genre and compete with its peers, it needs to be particularly good or have features which don't exist in others.

This is by far the largest category of games. They can contain new features which haven't been seen before but the essence of the game already exists.

The GOOD:

- ✓ There are hard-core fans of particular genres who tend to want to play anything new that gets released in their favourite.

- ✓ Sticking to a tried and tested game mechanic and control method means anyone who has played similar games can instantly pick it up.

- ✓ You can 'borrow' neat features of other games in the same genre and combine them.

The BAD:

- ✗ There is instantly a lot of competition so your game has to be better than the others, or offer something theirs doesn't (which could simply mean a better price).

- ✗ Your game will be compared to others of the same type, no matter who made them.

- ✗ Taking an existing game type and coming up with a new twist that players enjoy can be difficult.

There are far too many games in this category to list examples, but even games like "Doom", the first person shooting game from id Software, wasn't the first of its kind. "Wolfenstein 3D" could be seen as its predecessor. Technically speaking there were 3D maze games that allowed the player to wonder around in a 3D environment before that, but they weren't what we would now called an FPS shooter.

Many think "Mario Brothers" was the first proper platform game, but "Donkey Kong" was around in 1981. Even that isn't technically the first platform game as "Space Panic" was released to arcades in 1980.

A new type of game

This is the 'golden goose' for game developers; coming up with a new concept and game which hasn't been done before.

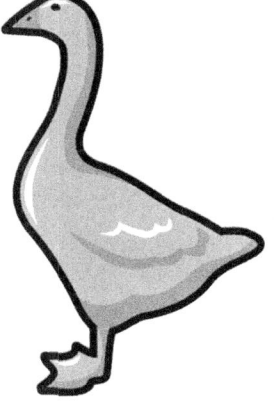

Big studios often steer clear of new ideas due to the risk involved if it turns out to be a flop and the potential to lose huge budgets. In recent years, the budgets given to triple 'A' games have grown astronomically, which is something they don't want to gamble with. It is said that "Grand Theft Auto V" cost over $240 million to make. "Call of Duty: Modern Warfare 2" apparently cost $250 million.

The GOOD:

- ✓ If you create a new game which gets popular, the world is your oyster when it comes to future projects and opportunities.

- ✓ Live forever as the person who invented something new.

The BAD:
- Coming up with something entirely new is incredibly difficult. Even when you think you have invented a new genre or type of game, you can later find that something similar has previously been released.

- Anything good will be copied and remade by others (see 'remakes' previously).

The big publishers prefer to stick to tried-and-tested games, which is why you see so many releasing sequels, expansion packs or similar games to ones which have already made lots of money and have a proven track record.

This is an area where the indie devs (independent game developers) can break out with that solid gold idea and take a chance on something new or different.

A quick quiz

Try answering the following multiple-choice questions based on ideas and game concepts. Answers are at the bottom of the page (so don't cheat!).

Question 1:
Not all games have a story, but those that do should try to ensure they do which of the following?

    A. Make the story the main part of the game with very little interaction with the player.
    B. Create the game first and think up a story to tack on afterwards.
    C. Balance the game's story with plenty of player interactivity.

Which category would you put the following games into?

Question 2: "Pac-Man" (1980)
    A. Remake   B. Existing genre   C. New concept

Question 3: "Call of Duty: Black Ops"
    A. Remake   B. Existing genre   C. New concept

Question 4: "The Last of Us: Remastered"
    A. Remake   B. Existing genre   C. New concept

Answers:			
1.C	2.C	3.B	4.A

The BIG questions

For every game you make, there are some important questions you have to ask.

This is what I like to call the

of game making, and should be decided upon early on in your planning phase.

Who...?

One of the biggest questions you must ask yourself when making a game is,

"who is this game aimed at?"

Who will actually play your game? The genre and theme may well influence this decision. For example, it is probably a bad idea to create a horror game for young children, or a skateboarding game for the elderly. The device it will run on and the controls available may also play a factor. The wider your audience the larger your market, but playing it too safe and trying to please everyone can also have drawbacks where nobody feels it is aimed at them.

What...?

Another big question is,

"what is the aim of the game?"

Is it to finish a story, complete missions, reach the last level, get the highest score, collect all of the items, survive the longest, etc...? This is something we will cover in more detail later on in the chapter 'Psychology'. There are some games which might appear not to have an aim initially, i.e. they can be played forever with no end, but there must still be a point to playing.

Why...?

The third big question is,

"why would people keep playing the game?"

Is there something to keep them coming back for more? This is also known as 'replay value'.

If the game is based on your own idea you may want to think about a USP - unique selling point. This is something that makes your game different to all others and is a big reason why people will buy it, play it, and keep playing it.

Games don't have to have a USP. In fact, many clones and sequels without a single original concept have been commercially successful but a USP does make it easier to promote and is usually what makes independent games stand out against the huge budget competition who won't take risks with untested ideas or concepts.

If your game has no end (like many puzzle games) or is quite short, it is important that players want to play it again.

How...?

The last big question is,

"how cutting-edge will your game be?"

Having a game take advantage of the most up-to-date hardware running on superfast, top-of-the-range computers can give it a serious **'wow'** factor, but it will only be playable by a small number of people.

If you make your game run on even the lowest specification computer then your potential market audience is huge but people may think it is too simple and it might lose realism. You may also have trouble giving your game the features and polish you would like if low end computers cannot cope with them.

You should also consider future versions of your game on other platforms. If a game is a run-away success, you will probably want to release it for as many devices as possible. Getting it running on platforms with a lower specification is easier if it doesn't require huge amounts of processing power.

Many games offer the ability to switch off features which aren't important to the gameplay and merely improve things like the visuals, for example motion blur, particles, lighting effects or more realistic shadows. Ideally your game will run on slow machines but automatically take advantage of modern, fast processors and expensive graphics cards if they are available, but this can be difficult to develop and take much longer - even requiring you to duplicate graphics and other resources your game uses at different quality levels.

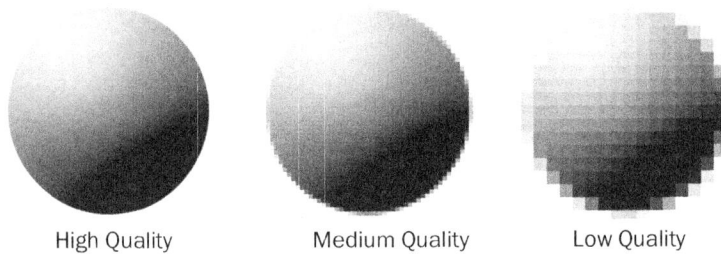

High Quality   Medium Quality   Low Quality

This doesn't just refer to PC's either. There is quite a difference between low end and high end mobile devices like smartphones and tablets. With the commercial availability of modern virtual reality (VR) and augmented reality (AR) equipment, there are some big differences between high end and low end versions of those too. Even consoles from the same company and released in the same generation can support different features, for example the PlayStation 4 and the PlayStation 4 Pro.

A tip for you:
Aiming your game at the middle to low range of computers or devices is probably easiest and a good place to start. It also opens it up to a large market share without losing or compromising too many features.

A quick quiz

Try answering the following multiple-choice questions based on this chapter. Answers are at the bottom of the page.

Question 1:
Which of the following is a possible 'aim' of a game?

- A. Finish the story.
- B. Get the highest score.
- C. Beat other players.
- D. All of the above.

Question 2:
What does U.S.P. stand for when talking about why people would play a game?

- A. Under Sold Performance.
- B. Unique Selling Point.
- C. Up Scaled Pixels.

Question 3:
A drawback of making your game playable on even the lowest specification hardware is...

- A. It will never win any awards.
- B. People outside of your target market will play it.
- C. The hardware may not support the features you want

Answers:		
1.D	2.B	3.C

Psychology

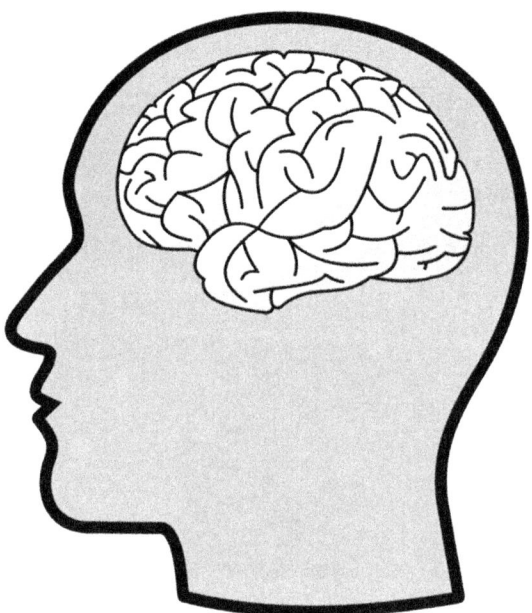

A little knowledge of psychology can help a lot when building a game.

Knowing about human behaviours along with the needs and wants of players can help you draw people into the game and give them a more enjoyable experience. Never forget, keeping your players happy, interested and entertained is why they play video games in the first place.

This has the side-effect of learning about yourself, why you like to play certain games and why you keep going back to them.

The aim

Let's start with the aim of the game. There needs to be something to achieve, e.g. a reward. This doesn't always mean finishing the game or concluding the story. Some games have no end such as puzzle games or MORPG's (Multi-user Online Role Playing Games like "World of Warcraft") but they will still have at least one aim.

This could be to unlock trophies or levels, to beat high scores or finishing times - either the player's own, their friend's or players from around the world. Or it could be just to stay alive for as long as possible, like "Temple Run" or "Flappy Bird". If you have a game with nothing to aim for, there is no incentive for players to return to the game to continue or perform better than their previous sessions. They won't feel like they have achieved anything while they are playing it and the whole thing can seem pointless.

Remember, there will be so many other video games released alongside yours, and the competition is so huge, that you need your players to want to complete your missions, beat your scores, or build your city instead of playing those other games.

A scary fact: If you released a game on the "Steam" platform in 2022 you would be competing with 10,963 other new games that year, on that one platform alone!

If you build it...

A lot of games rely on a human desire to build or create something. This can include solving something by putting pieces of a puzzle together or solving a mystery. The sense of achievement is the reward.

"Minecraft's" popularity is based on this. The enjoyment of creating your own structures far outweighs any of the other game elements for a lot of people.

Sharing your creations with friends or the world can also be a huge bonus to players. The level creation tools for games like "Doom" and "Unreal Tournament" were hugely popular. The PlayStation 3 game "Little Big Planet" from Media Molecule had 6 million user created levels by January 2012. In the first 11 days after Super Mario Maker 2 was released for the Nintendo Switch, 2 million user created levels had been uploaded.

There are exceptions though, such as "Tetris" which is probably the first example of a game where you are rewarded for destroying pieces of a puzzle. "Bejewelled" (and it's many clones) uses this idea too. Another modern day example would be "Angry Birds" which combines the destruction of buildings as one aim, with the unlocking of levels (and achieving those elusive 3 stars) as another aim.

Another Golden Goose

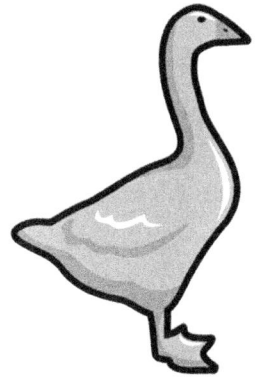

Addiction is another golden goose for game makers but it is difficult to pinpoint what would make people feel a need to return to your game. Of course, this also differs from person to person.

For some games the desire to finish it is compulsive, either by completing the story or all of the missions.

For others it may be to try and beat the player's own best scores or those of friends. Community gaming has always been huge since the dawn of video games where friends want to beat friends, get further, obtain a higher score or reach a higher level. Even games where players collaborate to reach a goal usually have some sense of competition.

In some games it is escapism that appeals to players. Becoming another character - a hero or even an anti-hero performing actions which they cannot do in real life is the draw. This is especially true when it is done in a multiplayer universe where they can meet others as a fictional persona and present themselves any way they like.

Who wouldn't want to be a fearsome knight, a wizard, an explorer or a warrior princess?

Where will it all end?

A decision also needs to be made whether you would be happy for someone to complete your game and stop. Completing a game and stopping is okay if it takes enough time that players feel satisfied at the end. You will always get those who play through games more than once if they enjoyed it, but offering alternate methods of finishing is always a bonus and can certainly make hard-core gamers want to experience them all, multiplying the time they spend playing your game.

Having optional tasks to complete also adds value for players. One example is to include side-missions which aren't necessary for the main story. Another is finding collectables and discover 100% of each level. The "Lego" games are particularly good at this and include a huge amount of collectable characters, side-missions and hidden items which completists love to replay to get that seemingly impossible 100% score. Being able to continue where your character is killed off makes it easy for players to want to give it "one more try".

The alternative is that there is no end so they can continue coming back forever (in theory). There is always a risk of the game becoming boring though so variation is key - even some sort of random element to make it continually different each time they play. This is where dynamic or "procedurally generated" levels can help.

Your mission, should you choose to accept it...

Challenge your players.

Knowing your target players is important to make the game challenging enough to ensure they want to play. It is another balancing act so your game is not too easy (i.e. boring) and not too difficult (i.e. frustrating), but there must be a challenge and it must stretch the player. This can be mentally with things like puzzles, or through dextrous skills like speed or accuracy.

Don't be afraid if it takes the average player 8 to 10 attempts to complete something important, especially if they get progressively better at the task each time and the reward is worth it. Overcoming the challenge is where the sense of achievement comes in, which itself can be addictive.

BUT be aware that this is where having random elements can be a potential downfall. Normally, some randomness can help make play varied and different every time, but if a player is struggling to complete a task and it keeps changing every time they retry, it can quickly lead to frustration and "rage quitting". If doing the same thing multiple times sometimes works and sometimes doesn't, players will get annoyed.

A tip for you:

The first few minutes of any game can be the deciding factor whether the player will continue playing or give up.

Try to make this as interesting and compelling as possible. Draw them in. Set up the story (if you have one). It's good to create some mystery and pose questions which they will want to find the answers to. Throw them a bone and let them obtain something that gives them that quick sense of achievement.

Give them a taste of what is in store but don't give the plot away. You might even want to class your first level like a movie trailer where they tease the viewer with things that might happen later on.

A good exercise is to think of a few games you have enjoyed playing in the past, and then think of reasons why you kept returning to them to keep playing.

The human element

Multiplayer games, where you compete or team up with other human players adds another element. The game sessions will always be different which hopefully removes the worry of repetitiveness that often occurs when playing with/against computer controlled players.

In days-gone-by having multiple players in a game meant you all needed to be sat in front of the same arcade machine or TV with a controller each. Now-a-days players can be across the other side of the globe with no lagging (delays) to the gameplay.

It does however open up a can of worms when it comes to matching players of similar abilities. Nobody enjoys joining a game which others have been playing for months and constantly beat you. Equally it soon becomes boring if you keep easily beating everyone else. One way around this is to include a single player mode against a progressively difficult computer opponent so the player can practice and become fluent with controls before moving on to playing human counterparts.

Don't underestimate the power of 'bragging' too. Even if your game doesn't allow playing against other humans directly, purely having the ability to post a global high-score or compare your progress with friends can give incredible replay value and lead to friendly tournaments.

Thinking differently

When it comes to creating any kind of software, you have to be aware that computers think differently to us humans.

"Pretty obvious", you may say but it is amazing how many people try to make the computer perform a job as a human would do it. This can lead to either failing miserably or using up lots of unnecessary time and resources.

Efficient and fast running code is essential for games. Keeping it as simple as possible is important too making it less prone to errors and easier to debug if problems do occur. Unnecessary and overly complex systems have been the downfall of many applications.

Think of a dishwasher

If you were building a dishwasher, would you make it with two arms that picked up dishes and scrubbed them in a bowl of hot water like a human does?

Or would you build a box to hold the dishes with powerful water jets to clean them?

The first method would be a LOT more expensive to make, it's a lot more complicated and therefore prone to failure, and it would be much less efficient than the second. The second method is better for an automated system.

Generally speaking, computer games can be some of the most power intensive software available using up as much CPU, graphics processing power and memory that they can grab - especially when compared to running applications software.

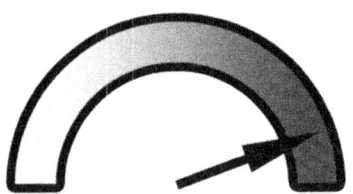

For example, if you create a spreadsheet application most people won't notice (or care) if a function takes a few milliseconds longer than it could to complete, but in a game where those calculations could be running hundreds or even thousands of times per second, that can mean the difference between 'smooth' and 'frustrating stutters'.

The more streamlined and efficient a game is programmed, the quicker and better it will run. Modern games really do try to push the hardware they are running on to their limits, whether that is PC's, consoles or mobile phones. You only need to read the reviews of some modern games to see how annoyed players get when games don't run as smoothly or as efficiently as they expect.

When I started programming it was on old 8 bit home computers - the first computers available to the public to have in their homes.

The memory in these computers was measured in low kilobytes - not megabytes or gigabytes like today. The processors had a speed of a few megahertz rather than the gigahertz processors now.

Average CPU Transistors (x 1 million) by Year

With such small amounts of memory and slow processors you had to write software that was efficient. You developed shortcuts for storing things in memory and cherished every byte. It could be said that many of today's programmers have been spoiled by the abundance of speed and resources in modern computers so may have fallen into the habit of writing code which is bloated, using more resources than they need. Just look at how much storage space some modern games take up, even for mobile devices.

If you really want to push your game making skills to the limits then I would recommend trying to write something for those old machines, or even modern day microcontrollers as a test to see if you can.

Pick a card

Here is a practical example of thinking differently.

Take the simple idea of a card game. The first thing you need to work out is how to shuffle and deal the cards.

Give a deck of cards to a human and this is what will most likely happen:

1) Mix up the cards by taking random quantities of them and changing the order in which they sit in the deck. Repeat this step until satisfied that the cards are mixed sufficiently.

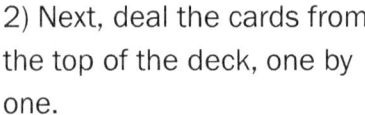

2) Next, deal the cards from the top of the deck, one by one.

A computer could do it this same way but it would be very inefficient, wasting time and resources. Let's see the process needed to emulate human shuffling and dealing by a computer. Afterwards you will see how you can do it much more efficiently in your own games.

34

Pick a card, like a human

For this example (and for simplicity) we will use a deck with only 6 cards and store them in an 'array' which you can think of as a big stack of storage slots, each one containing one card.

To shuffle them up like a human we could take a chunk of cards, say the contents of compartments 1 to 3, and move them to the end. To do this there are 3 steps:

1) Move cards 1 to 3 into a temporary array/store

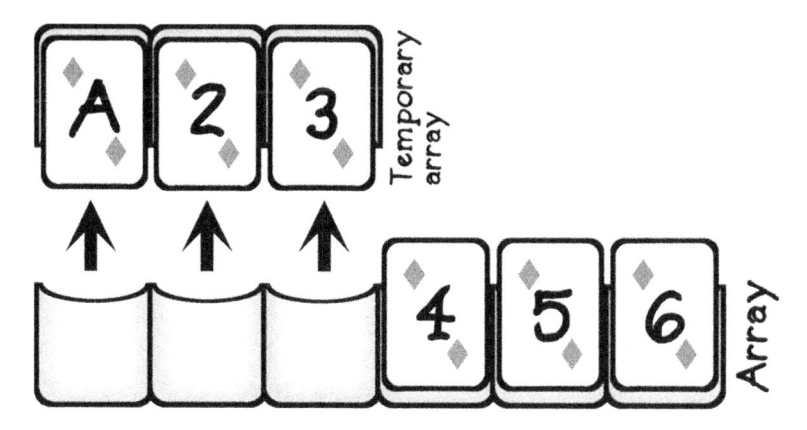

2) Move the cards from compartments 4 to 6 into 1 to 3

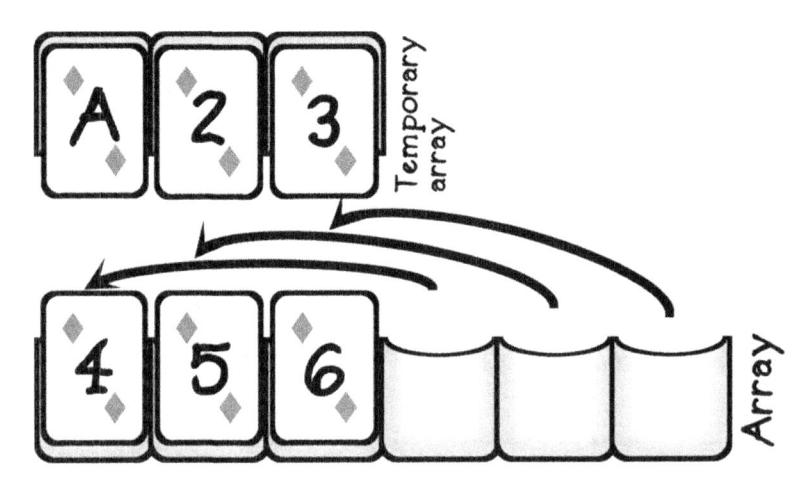

3) Finally move our temporary array cards back into compartments 4 to 6.

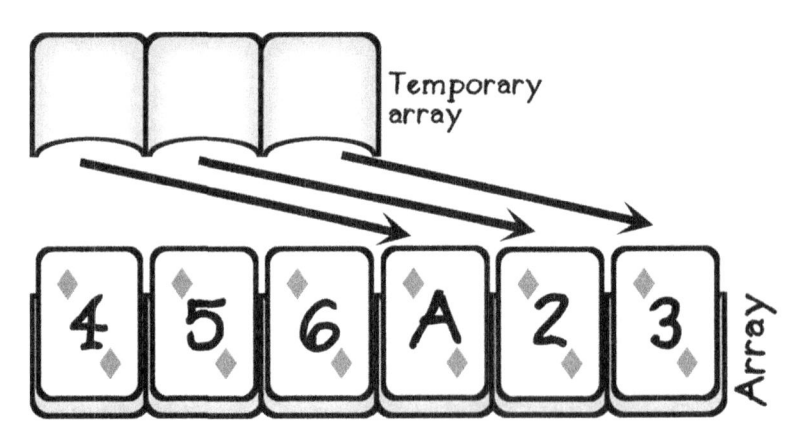

This may not seem like too much work but consider this with a full deck, using different sized chunks to make it more random, and repeating it until you are sure they are mixed up enough.

To deal the cards we could take a card from the top, move all the other cards up and then shorten the array by 1,

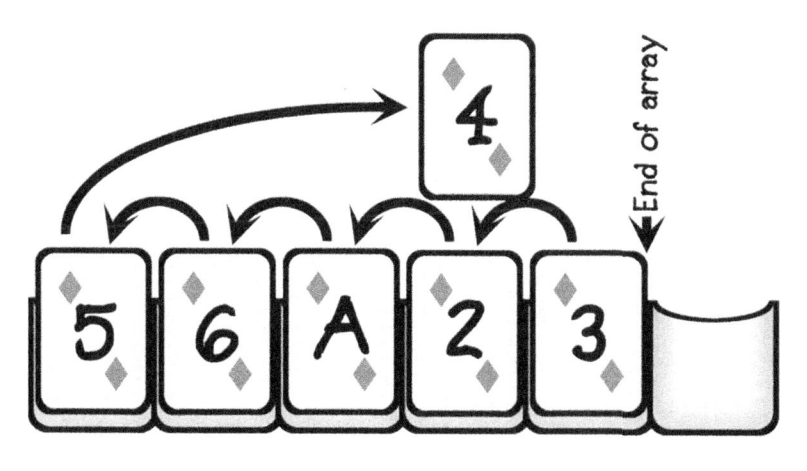

Or... we could take it from the top and keep a variable which tells us where the new top of the deck is,

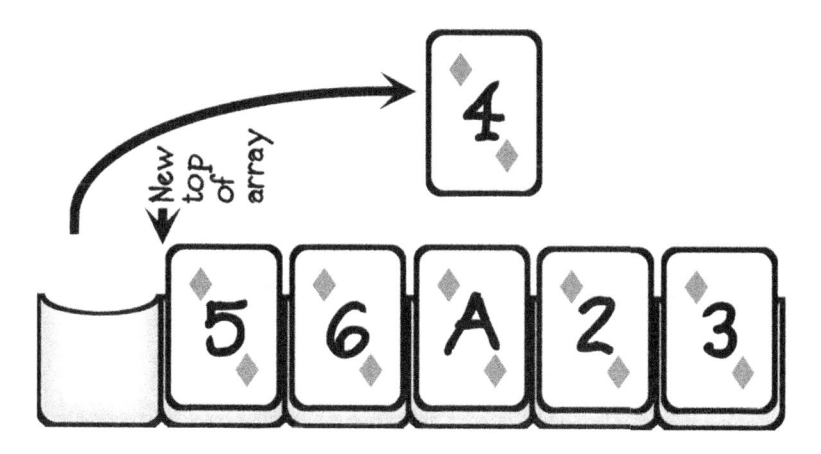

Or... better still, it would be easiest to take the last card in the array (i.e. dealing from the bottom of the deck - compartment 6) and then shorten the array by one each time until they are all gone.

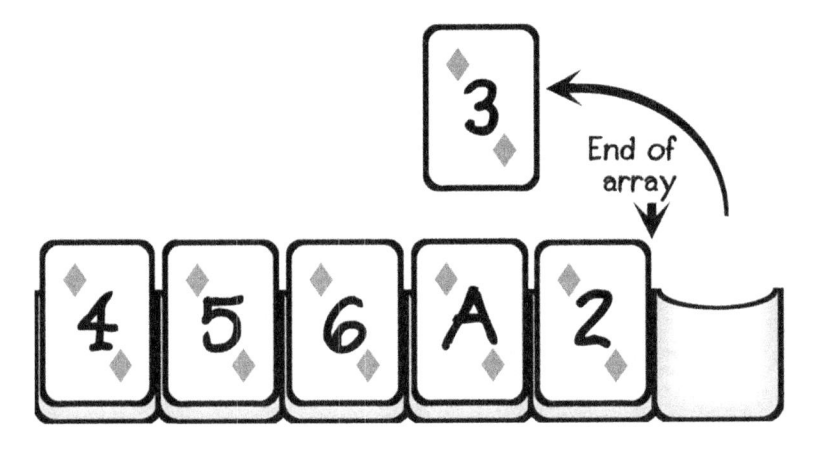

This isn't really how a human would deal the cards (from the bottom of the deck) but they can, and it wouldn't make much difference to the randomness in the order of cards. It also makes managing the array much easier as you only need to keep note of the length of the array.

You can probably already see that there is a complex number of steps involved and additional storage required (i.e. the temporary array) in order for the computer to shuffle and deal like humans do. Now let's see how we can improve this process for computers.

Pick a card, like a computer

If we rethink the problem in a way which is friendlier to how computers work we can make the process run much faster, using less memory and resources.

Take our array again but this time we have no need to shuffle the cards.

Instead let us deal a card from a random position, say compartment 4.

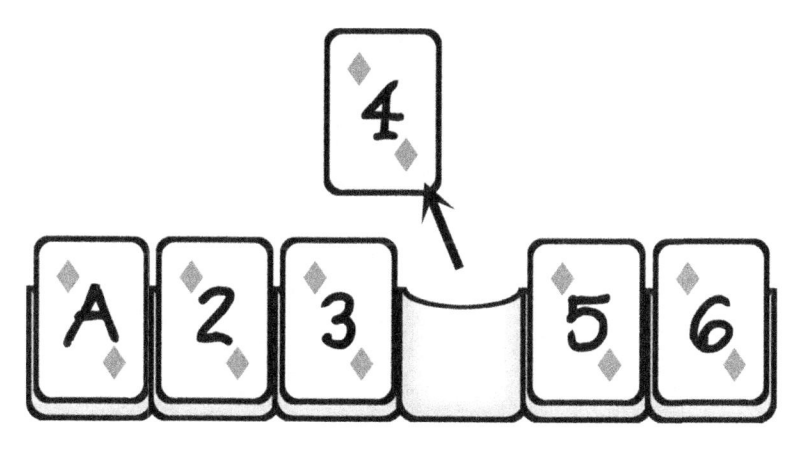

We don't need that compartment now but it is difficult to destroy a compartment in the middle of an array, so instead we simply copy the last item (from compartment 6) into the gap (compartment 4) and shorten the array by one.

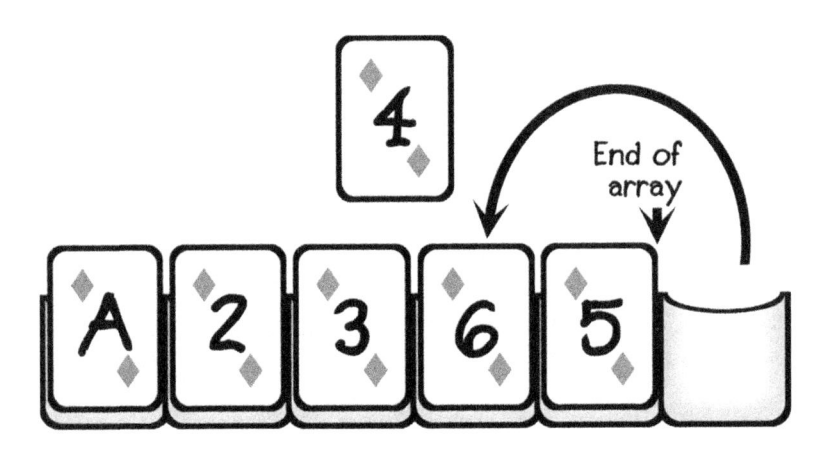

We can repeat randomly choosing a card and filling the gap with the last card until all of the array items are gone. When all of the cards are dealt you can reset everything quickly back to the start as if using a new deck.

I was quite young when I came up with this method for dealing cards in a game and was really pleased with myself... until I did some research and found out it was already being used by other programmers.

Oh well. Once you come up with a clever routine like this one for dealing cards, you will find you can re-use it. For example, instead of playing cards we could have a bank of questions in a trivia game. This same method could be used to choose questions at random and ensure the same questions aren't asked again until they have all been used and everything is reset.

Creating your own library of useful routines is really handy and can speed up development time for future projects.

A quick quiz

Try answering the following multiple-choice questions. Answers at the bottom of the page.

Question 1:
Some tasks are performed better by computers than humans. Which of these is done better by a computer?

- A. Physical tasks.
- B. Artistic creation.
- C. Mathematical problems.

Question 2:
Sorting numbers is a common chore. Which do you think would be able to perform that task most efficiently?

- A. A computer.
- B. A human.
- C. Neither.

Question 3:
Why was the computer method of shuffling and dealing cards more efficient for a computer than the human method?

- A. It sees all of the cards at once rather than individually.
- B. It doesn't require a temporary store for moving cards and uses fewer steps.
- C. It can predict which card will be dealt next.

Answers:		
1.C	2.A	3.B

Interactive devices

Your target gaming device can make a big difference to what games will work, and how the player will interact with them.

For example, if you are designing for a games console with a joypad then a game which tries to act as a typing tutor would not work well. Similarly, a fast fighting game requiring lots of buttons for kicking, punching and blocking won't work well on a touch screen device (even though some developers do try!).

It isn't just game mechanics and interaction which are affected by your target device. Limitations and optimizations to make your game run quickly and smoothly will differ. Learn as much as you can about your chosen machines.

An example is the Android operating system, and some of its graphics libraries which work better if your image sizes are to the power of 2. This means their height and width could be 2, 4, 8, 16, 32, 64, 128 etc. pixels in size. The system may let you use any size of image but they will often put aside a memory block the next size up to store it, so an image of 68 pixels square will end up using memory the size of a 128 pixel square image.

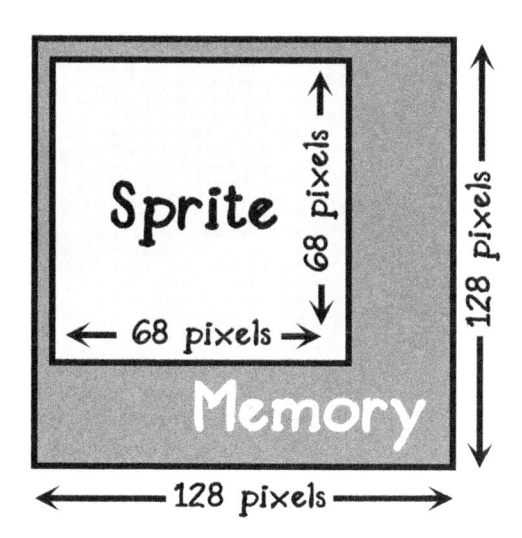

It might not seem like much on small sprites like this, but imagine hundreds of larger sprites, or texture maps for 3D objects. All of that assigned and wasted memory adds up and could slow things down.

Need input

Touch screens, gamepads, motion controllers (both physical and camera based), mice and keyboards... It is incredibly helpful to know how these things work so you can take full advantage of them and know about their drawbacks and how they might affect your gameplay. This includes the technical and electronic aspects as you'd be surprised how often that knowledge can help.

Most people use these devices without a second thought. They just expect them to work as they always have, but with so many different manufacturers and technologies at play, what works fine on your equipment might actually be a problem for some of your players.

Ghost in the Machine

Many years ago I encountered great frustration when writing keyboard control routines for games. Until I researched how the hardware side of keyboards work, this problem drove me to distraction - and I am certainly not the only one.

More expensive keyboards usually suffer less than cheap ones, BUT most still have some 'ghosting' and/or 'masking' problems. Let me explain what these are and why they happen in an overly simplified manner.

Ghosting

Here is a typical representation of a keyboard. I know the layout is wrong and most people don't have a key labelled 'Fire', but bear with me. Consider these buttons as the 'mapped' controls in your game for moving a character.

This is what the circuitry of the keyboard would actually look like underneath. Each button is a switch on a 'matrix' or grid of wires, known as the keyboard matrix. When you close a switch by pressing a button it links a horizontal line to a vertical line. By testing each line you can tell which are linked and therefore which buttons are being pressed.

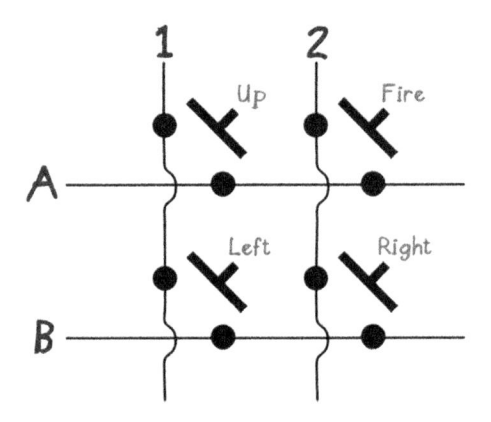

Here is what happens when a single key is pressed - let's say the 'Left' key.

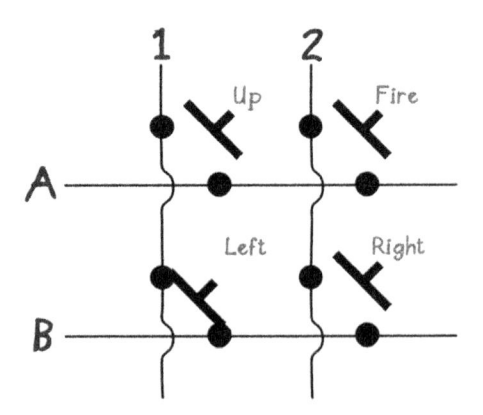

Row 'A' is scanned first and a check is made to see if it is connected to column '1'. It isn't, so we know the 'Up'

key isn't being pressed. Then row 'A' and column '2' is tested. No link there so the 'Fire' key is not being pressed.

Then the next row 'B' is tested against column '1' and we find a link so know the 'Left' key is pressed. Finally row 'B' and column '2' is tested. No key presses there.

Let's try two keys depressed at the same time – the 'Up' key and the 'Right' key. Perhaps our game character is jumping to the right.

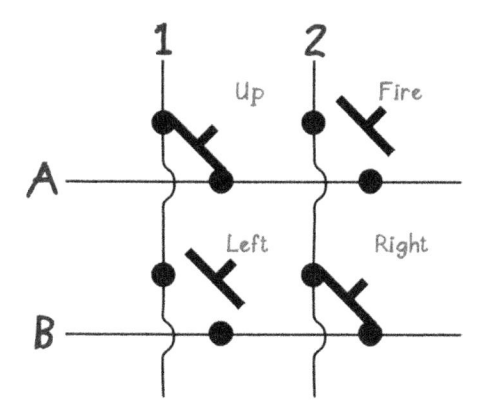

Just as before, we test each row against each column in turn. We can see that lines 'A' and '1' are connected (which we will call 'A1' from now on) so we know 'Up' is being pressed.

When we test row 'B' we find that 'B2' is connected so we know that 'Right' is being pressed. Simple so far.

Now let's try three keys pressed at the same time. Our character could be jumping to the right and shooting at the same time. This is where the problem starts.

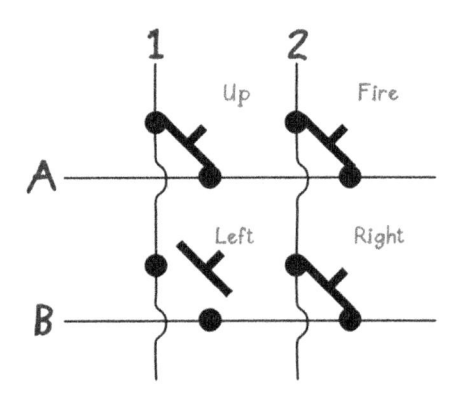

First we test row 'A' and see that it connects to column '1' and column '2'. 'A1' is 'Up' and 'A2' is the 'Fire' key.

Now for row 'B' and we see it connects to column '2' - the 'Right' key.

Do you see the problem yet? There is an extra link which you could call a 'short circuit'.

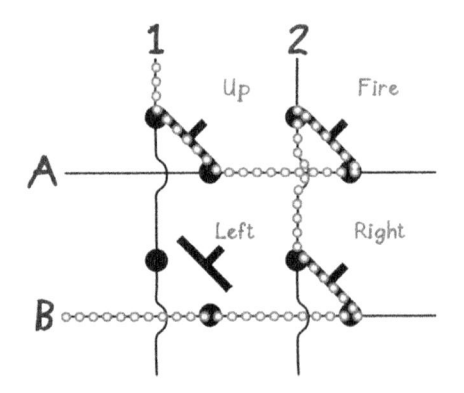

If you follow row 'B' you will see a connection route through to column '1', demonstrated here with the dotted line. It's a long route, but it's still a link so our system would think that 'B1' (the 'Left' key) is also depressed - a ghost key!

Masking

Masks are just as scary as ghosts. If you take our three button example there is an added possible problem.

If you now press the 'Left' button while the others are still depressed, it will not matter because it already thinks the left button is held down.

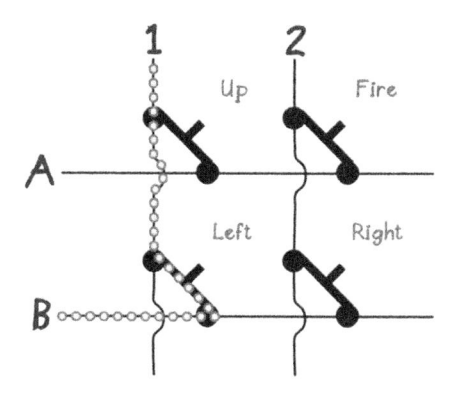

If you then release the 'Fire' button the system will think it is still being held down due to the new 'short circuit' shown by the dotted line below.

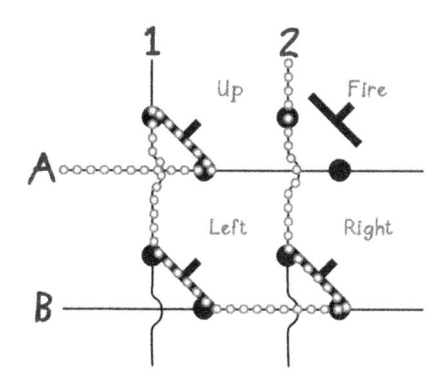

You can see why it thinks that 'A2' is still being depressed.

This is what's known as a 'mask' - a button which it hasn't recognised has been released.

Fixing ghosts and masks

Modern keyboards are made to detect these 'ghost' and 'mask' key presses and try to prevent them.

Often they still cannot determine which are the real keys being pressed so they just prevent any more keys on the same matrix lines from being recognised. It's like a 'first come, first served' scenario so the first key pressed takes priority. The keyboard may also start beeping to tell you there is a problem.

Good keyboard designers tend to move commonly pressed keys onto different matrix lines so there is less of a chance one will be blocked because the other was pressed first.

There is a way to fix the problem by adding diodes into the matrix.

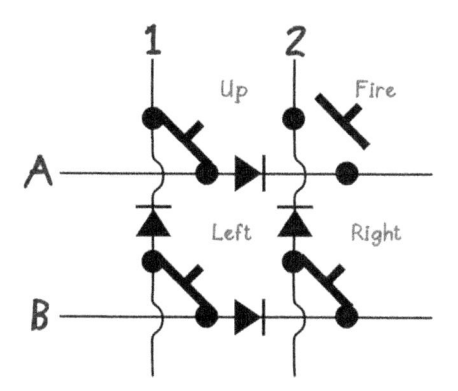

These prevent the short circuits from occurring by only allowing the tests to flow one way through the switches. This would rectify the original three button problem. It does however make the keyboard more expensive and more complex to make.

The conclusion?

As you cannot determine whether the player is using a budget keyboard, or which matrix lines particular keys are on, the only way you can ensure that they will be able to effectively play your game would be to allow them to redefine the keys they use to play it.

Allowing the user to play using whatever keys they are comfortable with makes your software more accessible – which is always a good thing.

Touchy touchy

Like most technology, the way touch screens work has changed over the years to improve the experience for users and take advantage of new developments.

There are three main types of touch detection on screens. Some are more popular than others, some work better, and some are more expensive. All of these factors determine their popularity and where you might see them being used.

Resistive touch screens

These screens were used in early devices and can still be found in some low end devices now. They rely on two layers of conductive material which sit on top of the LCD display.

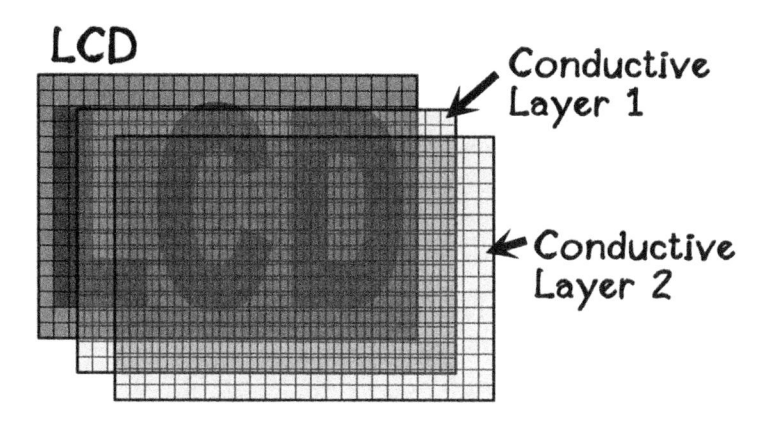

LCD

Conductive Layer 1

Conductive Layer 2

These two layers are slightly separated until a finger or stylus is pushed against the top later causing it to bend and touch the back layer. The screens detect where the touch has taken place and return the coordinates.

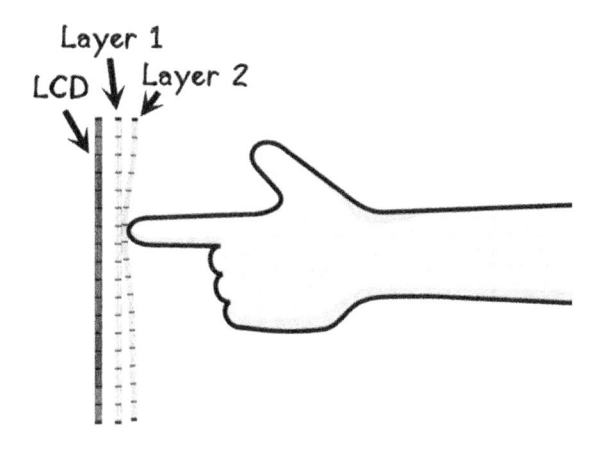

Layer 1
LCD Layer 2

The GOOD:
- ✓ Resistive touch screens were originally much cheaper to make than other types of touch screen.

- ✓ They will work through gloves or with anything to act as a stylus.

- ✓ They can be more resilient than other screens due to their slightly flexible nature.

The BAD:
- ✗ They aren't particularly accurate.

- ✗ You can only detect a single touch at a time - so no pinch zooming.

- ✗ As they require pressure to work, dragging across the screen can also be awkward.

Resistive touch screens are still used in some sat nav devices, ATM (automated teller machines) cash points and in industries where users may need to control machinery while wearing protective gloves, such as warehouses or engineering workshops. The price of manufacture is not really a factor any more.

Capacitive touch screens

These work by having a small electrical charge across the screen. When a conductive material touches the screen (such as our finger) it draws some of this electrical current and distorts the electrostatic field. This change can be measured by sensors to give a distance and converted into coordinates on the screen.

Original capacitive touch screens had electrodes in each corner and could only detect a single touch but modern capacitive screens have 'sensing' lines (horizontal lines) and 'driving' lines (vertical lines) and each point where they cross can be detected independently allowing multiple touches to be measured.

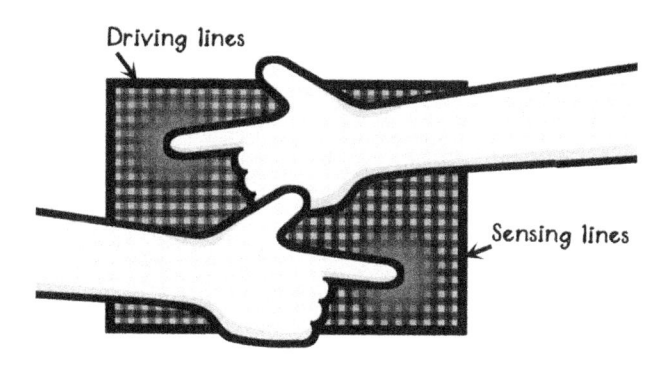

The GOOD:
- ✓ Modern capacitive screens can detect and track multiple touches at once, very quickly. Screens able to detect 5 simultaneous touches are not uncommon.

- ✓ They don't require a hard press so less effort is needed to drag or pinch.

- ✓ As there is no physical movement involved (unlike the resistive touch screens which require a bending layer) they are less likely to break or become less sensitive over time.

The BAD:
- ✗ Capacitive touch screens only work when touched with a conductive material like skin or conductive thread like you find in the fingertips of special touch screen gloves.

- ✗ Originally they were more expensive than resistive screens due to the more complicated technology involved, but their mass production now means this is not really an issue any more.

Capacitive touch screens are what you find in modern day smart phones, tablets, touch screen laptops (like many Chromebooks) and most high-end in-car entertainment systems that utilise a touch screen for control.

Optical touch screens

These screens are currently nowhere near as popular as the other two but worth a mention anyway. They work by sending light through a clear surface or over the top of it. When something touches the surface it either scatters or breaks the light which can be detected with sensors or cameras to tell where the touch takes place.

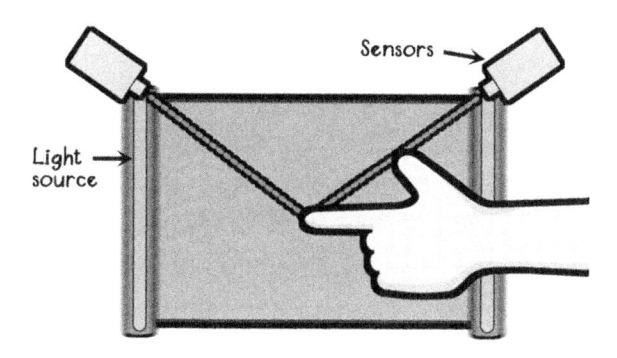

The GOOD:
- ✓ These screens can detect any object breaking or scattering the light, not just conductive ones.
- ✓ There is no electronics or anything embedded in the glass screen itself so in theory they can be made much bigger than other types of touch screen for a lower cost.

The BAD:
- ✗ They are prone to interference from other light sources.
- ✗ Multiple touches can be tricky to detect if they block each other from the sensor's point of view.

Touchy conclusion

Unless you are creating a game for a specific device you probably want to play it safe and make it work on as many as possible - thereby having a wider audience. Even though some screens (mainly tablets) can cope with around 10 simultaneous touches on their capacitive screens, others seem to have a maximum of around 5.

In my opinion, even expecting a user to be able to touch 5 things at once on a touch screen is too much (unless you are simulating a musical keyboard). This is partly due to the size of the screen. With that many touches your hands would block the majority of your view, but there is also no tactile feedback from touch screens. By 'tactile' I mean the user cannot feel the edge of a button or the movement or click of it being depressed. Unlike a physical button on a keyboard or joypad, you have to lift fingers off the screen to stop a touch being detected which makes it very easy to accidentally drift off your button areas and you end up missing them.

This is partly why I think touch screen games which simulate a joystick don't work particularly well as it is so easy to slide your thumb off the joystick area (or at least I do!). Personally, I think touch screens open up new and different ways of controlling games that we should take advantage of rather than trying to shoehorn traditional control methods into this newer interactive technology.

A quick quiz

Try answering the following multiple-choice questions on touch screens. Answers at the bottom.

Question 1:
Mobile gaming is a huge market with 95% of adults aged 16 to 34 owning a smartphone. The primary input on mobile devices is the touchscreen, but what sort of touchscreen do the vast majority have?

- A. Capacitive touch screens.
- B. Resistive touch screens.
- C. Optical touch screens.

Question 2:
In an environment such as a warehouse where users wear gloves, which type of touchscreen is most suitable for devices requiring input?

- A. Capacitive touch screens.
- B. Resistive touch screens.
- C. Optical touch screens.

Question 3:
Multi-touch screens are commonplace on mobile devices. Which feature relies on support for multi-touch functionality?

- A. Volume control up/down.
- B. Simulating a right mouse button.
- C. Pinch zooming a photo.

Answers:
1.A   2.B   3.C

The motion notion

There will always be a place for hand held or traditional control methods in games, such as joypads, joysticks, mice, keyboards and touchscreens. After all, nobody wants to be leaping about or waving their arms around on public transport!

But control methods where you can use your body to move around in a virtual world or control a character is something that has taken off hugely in recent years. They are wonderful for increasing a sense of immersion in a game. They can also be used to combine gaming and fitness or even physiotherapy. Training people who may have to work in dangerous places or situations can help to save lives too.

Virtual Reality

VR has been commercially available since the early 1990's from companies like Virtuality and CyberMaxx but it has taken until now for the processing power, technology and price to make it popular with home users. It consists of wearing a headset so screens can be shown in front of the user's eyes. They detect the angle or position of the head so the image is updated in line with the player's movement. I am bundling AR (that's Augmented Reality) in with VR as it overlays the virtual world on top of the real world but the principles can be the same.

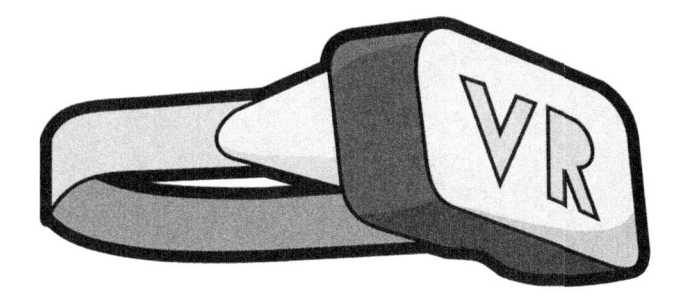

With Sony's PlayStation VR (formally called Project Morpheus), the Oculus Rift and Oculus Quest, the HTC Vive and Microsoft's HoloLens there are some big companies banking on it getting bigger and bigger in the years to come.

There are a growing number of games and applications available for these systems, and there is now a free and open standard they could all abide by to make developing software for them easier, called OpenXR.

The truth is you don't have to spend a fortune on hardware to develop some clever VR games. If you have a smart phone with a gyroscope (which most middle to top end phones do) then you can play Google Cardboard based VR games.

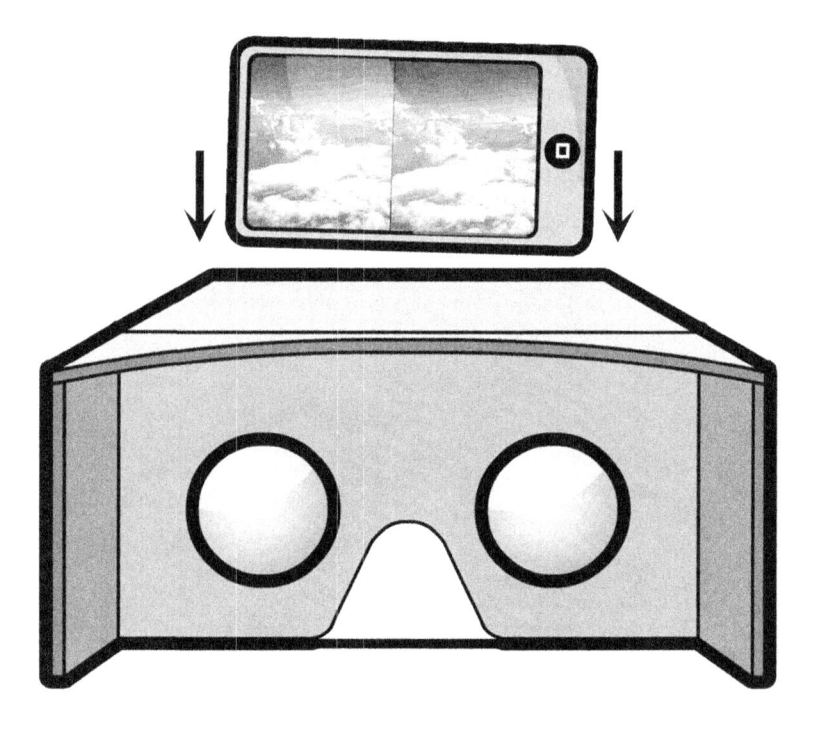

Google Cardboard started out as a simple and cheap cardboard frame to house your smartphone which does all of the hard work. You can buy them online for a few pounds/dollars or get a sturdy plastic one for a bit more. Writing software for it is reasonably easy using free tools/libraries. The screen on your phone is simply split into two, one side shows the left eye view and the other side shows the right eye view. Lenses focus and magnify the views for each eye. By using the built-in gyroscope you can turn your head and look around in any direction.

Google Cardboard works best when the smart phone has a high resolution screen and enough power to simultaneously render the two images quickly and smoothly at a decent frame rate.

The only issue is with interacting with the game. VR software I have written involves pointing your head at what you want to interact with, usually for a set amount of time. A countdown timer is shown and if it reaches zero while you are looking at something in your crosshairs then that item is selected. Move the crosshair away from it and the countdown timer resets.

If your phone has a magnetometer then some Google Cardboard headsets come with a magnetic button they can detect which can be used for selecting menu items, shooting, or anything you like.

Alternatively, you could use a cheap Bluetooth joypad or button to connect to your phone and control things that way. It's a very cost effective way to start developing your own Virtual Reality games.

Camera based motion

There are several methods of detecting movement based around a camera.

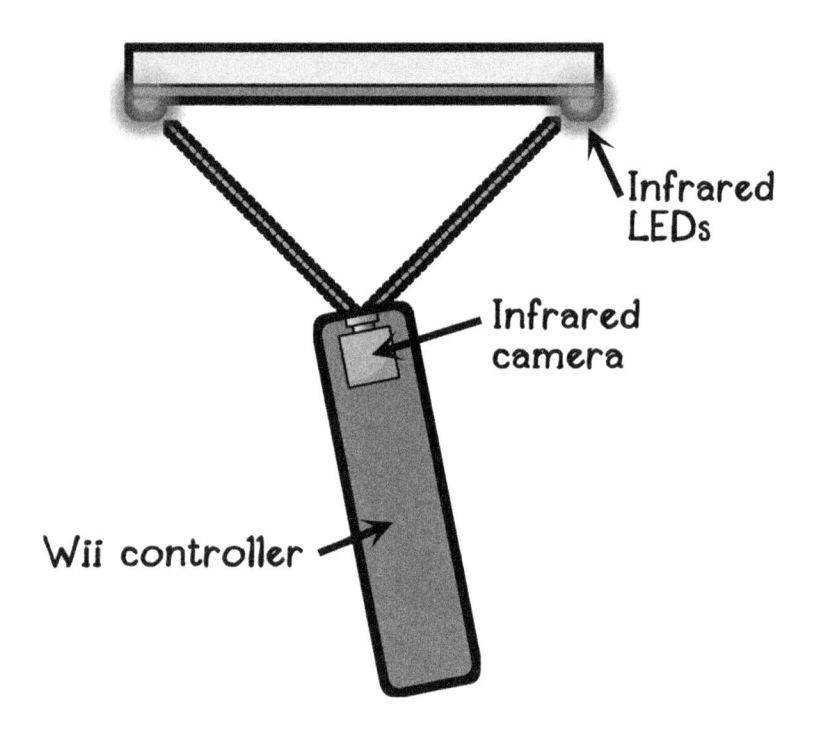

Infrared LEDs

Infrared camera

Wii controller

The Wii controller has a camera in it which can see the infra-red light from the fixed sensor bar. It uses this and accelerometers to detect the movement and rotation of the handset. A visible light filter on the camera blocks out everything but the infra-red light from the sensor bar making it easier to detect where the lights are and therefore where the handheld controller is pointing.

The PS4 uses a fixed camera system and a light on a handset to detect movement in 3D space. The PlayStation 3, 4 and 5 can also use a special PlayStation Move controller with a glowing sphere to quickly and accurately measure its placement and distance from the camera, along with inertial sensors, a three-axis accelerometer and three-axis angular rate sensor to track rotation and motion. By changing the colour of the sphere it supports up to 4 Move controllers at once with one camera.

PlayStation 4 controllers include a light built into its joypad. With a dual camera system for distance measurement, three-axis gyroscope and three-axis accelerometer inside the controller they can detect position, motion and rotation.

Infrared projector → ← Infrared depth sensor

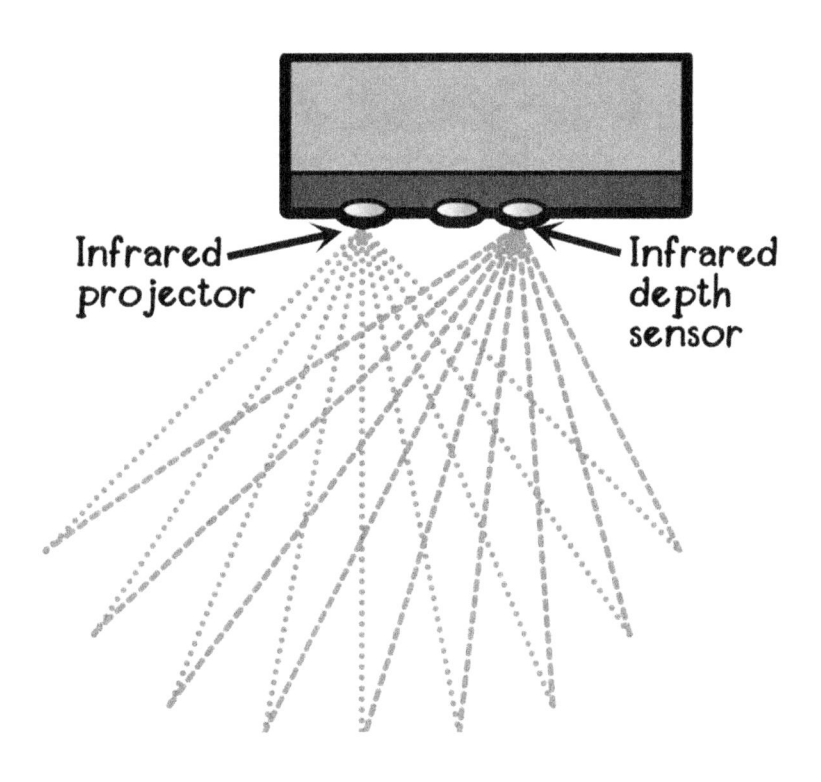

The Kinect camera system for the Xbox360 and Xbox One uses an infrared projector and separate infrared depth sensor to map the environment and players.

It is capable of mapping a skeleton onto the player and working out the positions of their physical joints. The original Xbox 360 version supports 2 players and can track the motion of up to 20 joints, whereas the Xbox One version supports 6 players and up to 25 joints. This enables the system to use the player's own body motion to control on-screen characters. Great for dancing games!

The formula

You might not want to hear this, but if you are going to code your own games, you will need mathematics.

You can get away without memorising formulas and advanced mathematical theory but you will need to know where to find them when you need them. And you probably will need them at some point if you are serious about writing your own efficient code.

There are programming libraries which can look after a lot of what you need, for example the mathematics involved in calculating 3 dimensional points in space for any 3D game can be very complex but if you use a pre-written library or SDK (software development kit) then hopefully that will look after it for you.

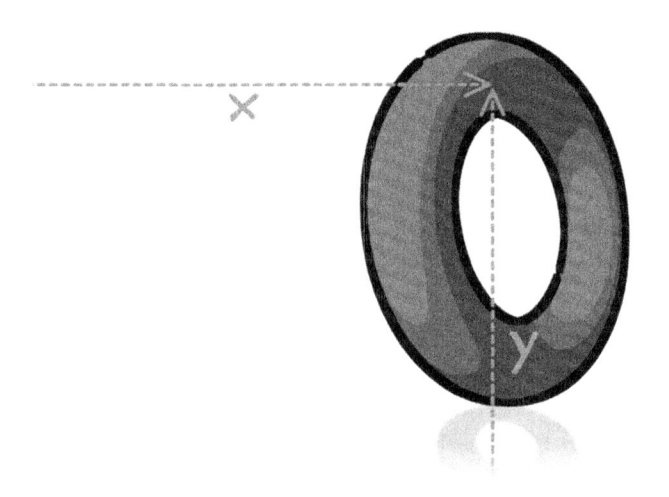

Learning a bit about what the maths is doing behind the scenes though can definitely be beneficial and you can use it to your advantage to find shortcuts to speed things up and make your game more efficient. For example, if you only use a couple of complicated maths functions it can use up lots of unnecessary space and even slow your game down if you include a huge pre-existing library containing hundreds of unused functions.

There will always be times when pre-built libraries can't help you so knowing some of the simple rules about trigonometry and Pythagoras will help you out.

Example 1 - travelling to the 3rd dimension

Let's get started with some basic 3D by creating a point in 3D space.

For that point to exist in our virtual world it needs a value in each of the 3 dimensions.

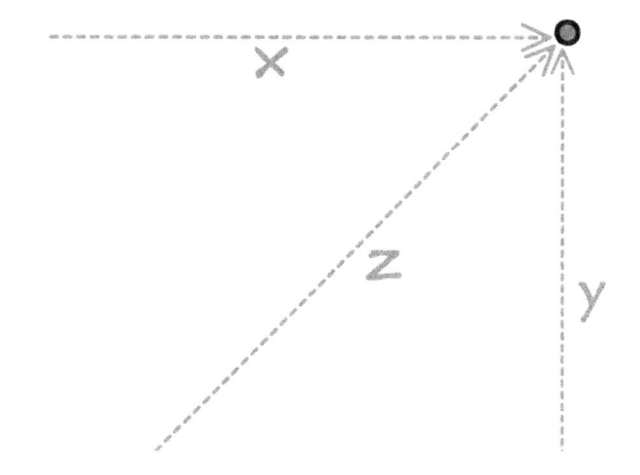

- the x axis (which tells us how far it is to the right),

- the y axis (telling us how far up it is, or how high),

- and the z axis (telling us how far back it is, away from us).

With these three values our point - which is known as a 'vertex' - can exist in 3D space.

Let's add 3 more. To make things simple we will make them all have the same value for the y axis so they all live at the same height. If our camera was at the same height we would see them all in a line so it is more useful to move our camera up and angle it down a little so we are looking slightly down at them.

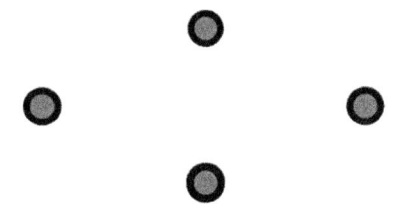

Now let's join them up with lines known as 'edges'. You can start to see our basic, flat 3D plane now.

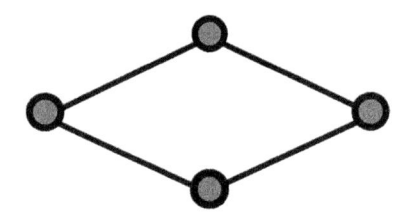

This is known as 'vector graphics' which create a 3D wireframe and was used in old 3D computer games like the 1983 "Star Wars" arcade machine, and "Battlezone" from 1980.

If we fill the area inside our wireframe edges then we have a 'face' or polygon. In this case, as our polygon has 4 edges it is a quadrilateral. Some 3D engines find it faster and easier to deal with 3 sided polygons so for efficiency you may need to look into this for the platform you are developing for.

You can quickly see how these basic principles can be used to build 3D objects on a 2D screen. By moving the vertices you can give the impression of a shape in 3D space, rotating or moving around in relation to the viewer – which can be thought of as a camera.

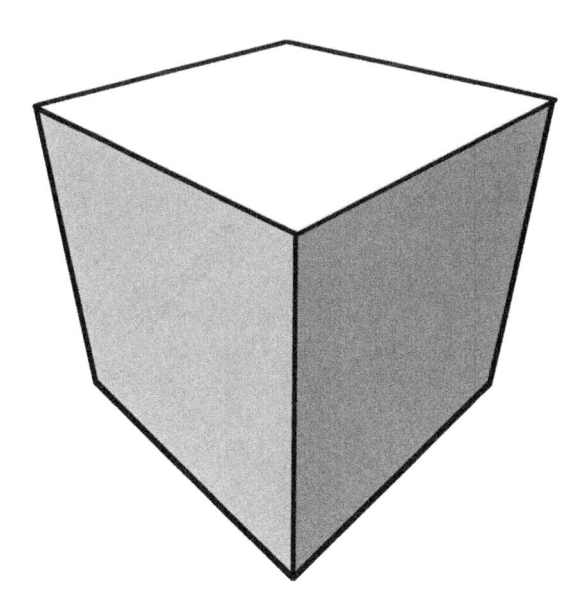

Just out of interest, in order to work out where a point or vertex would be when rotated around the axis you need to use trigonometry... but don't worry, I won't go into those formulas here.

The maths will start to get a little more complicated from here but the methods explained will hopefully help you understand what goes on 'under the hood' of most games.

Example 2 - when worlds collide

The vast majority of games involve detecting collisions of some sort. Whether this is between a character and a platform, a space ship and a rocket, a mouse pointer and an object, or between two puzzle pieces - collisions are an important thing to detect.

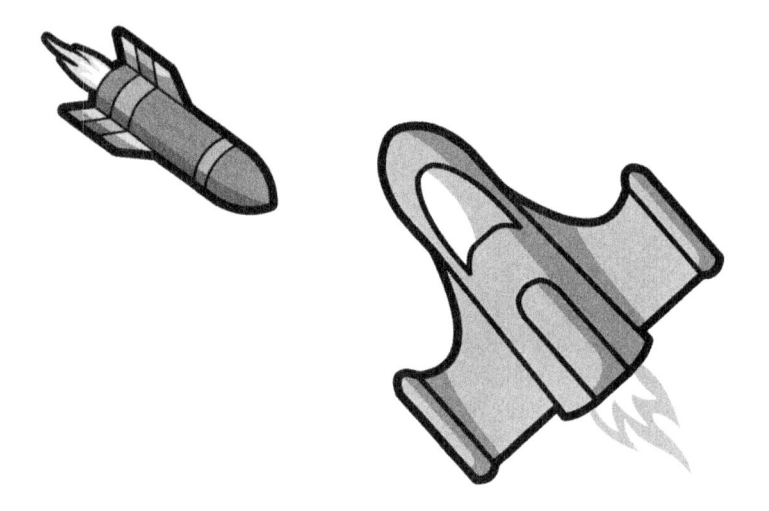

Again, some programming libraries look after this for you but may not cope with all eventualities so it is worth learning some of the basics. Their methods may also be overkill for what you need and you may be able to write something that works quicker and more efficiently yourself.

We're going back to the world of 2D games to make things easier but the principles apply in 3D too.

Let's say we have a nice square spaceship. It is unlikely but sometimes you can get away with using simple rectangular collision detection as it is fast and easy to check.

We know where the left, right, top and bottom edges of the spaceship are, and we know where the bullet is. We would simply check if the x and y coordinates of the bullet fall between the left edge and the right edge of the ship, and between the top edge and the bottom edge of the ship. If it does, we have a collision.

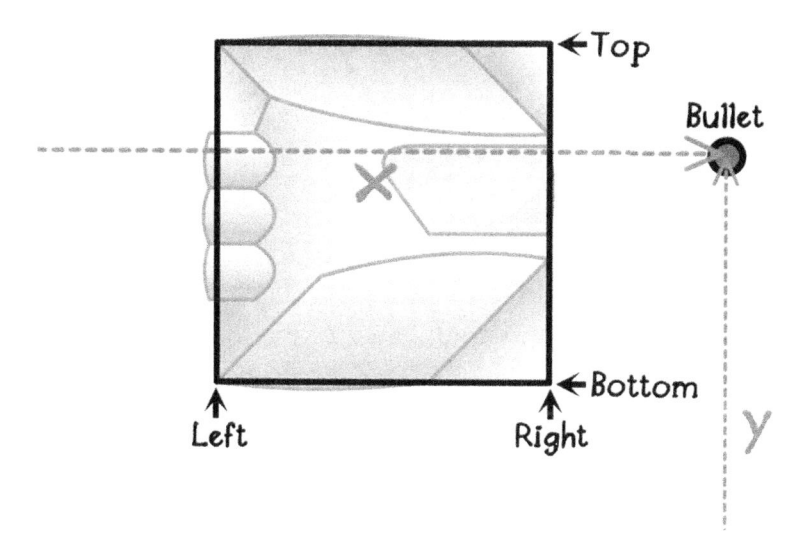

This isn't pixel perfect collision detection but for most games where the bullet is small and the spaceship isn't a really odd shape, it is good enough. In general terms, the quicker things move on the screen, the less accurate you need to be.

Now let's say we have a circular spaceship and we need to know if the bullet has hit it. This looks a lot more complicated but by using a little maths formula (specifically Pythagoras's theorem) we can work it out.

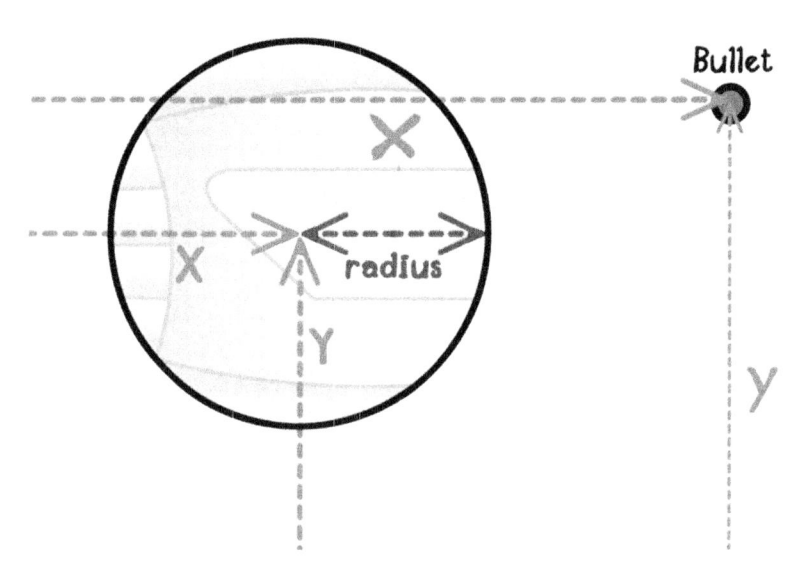

We have the x and y coordinates for the bullet and we have the x and y coordinates for the centre of the circle. We also know its radius (i.e. the distance from the centre of the circle to its edge). Imagine the centre of the circle and the bullet form a triangle where the distance between the x coordinates is known as the 'adjacent' side of the triangle, and the distance between the y coordinates is known as the 'opposite' side of the triangle. We need to find out the length of the 'hypotenuse' side of the triangle which will tell us how far away the bullet is.

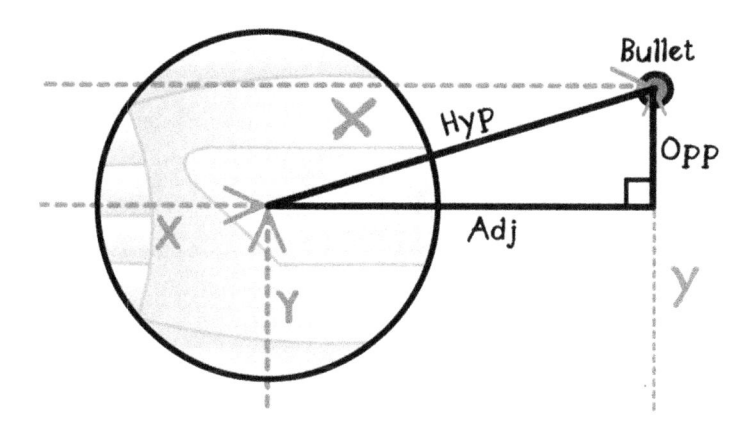

Pythagoras tells us that the distance between the two points can be found by using this formula:

$$distance^2 = (bulletx - cirlcex)^2 + (bullety - circley)^2$$

Having the squared value of the distance is no good so we need to find its square root, plus we can simplify the whole thing like this:

$$d = \sqrt{(bx - cx)^2 + (by - cy)^2}$$

Once we have the distance value it is just a case of working out whether the distance between the centre of the circle and the bullet is smaller than the distance between the centre of the circle and its edge, i.e. its radius. If it is, we have a collision.

If (the distance < the radius) then COLLISION!

The conclusion?

A lot of people struggle with maths so if you are one of them, don't panic! As I have said previously, a lot of software libraries used in gaming will do most of this work for you. It is definitely still worth knowing how they do it though.

I didn't really see the benefits of formulas and calculations like this until I started programming games. It is much easier to learn something if you can see the real life benefits and applications. Actually knowing how it can help you create something wonderful will help you to remember it better.

My advice... stick with it. It is worth it.

Make your own "fruit slice" game

In this section I am going to show you the basics of creating a "Fruit Slice" type game.

This type of game was made famous by the hugely popular "Fruit Ninja" game on mobile devices which was downloaded more than 1 billion times in its first 5 years. There are many, many variations, clones and copies around, slicing or chopping up all kinds of objects. It is a perfect example of a new type of game which took advantage of touch screens.

The concept is simple:

Various items of fruit are thrown onto the screen and the player has to slice them to win points.

There are usually some items you have to avoid (like bombs for some reason) and usually a clock or item limit you are playing against.

It works particularly well on touch screens because you can use your finger to slice up the fruit.

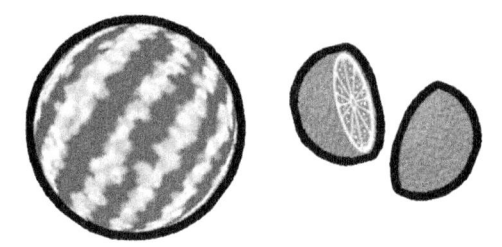

As explained at the start of this book, rather than giving you the source code for this game which will only work in one language and limit what platforms you can run it on, I will give you all the basic mechanics you need to build it in any language of your choice and for any device that you prefer.

The pseudo code will be shown to help you understand how it works and hopefully easily build it in whatever language you choose.

IMPORTANT: Make sure you read this chapter in its entirety first, before you start coding your own version so you understand how it works.

Hidden rules

You may not have noticed it when playing, but most of these fruit slice games have hidden rules to make it easier to code. Some may call this cheating, but it simplifies development and makes the game run more efficiently. Most importantly, it doesn't detract from the gameplay or fun.

For example:

- ✓ Our version will be in 2D to make coding it simpler, although the same methods could easily be used to make a 3D version.

- ✓ Each item of fruit is actually made up of two, pre-cut images that overlap each other to hide the cut.

- ✓ When you slice the fruit, it will always be cut through the middle no matter where you actually slice it.

- ✓ The fruit will always be round. This helps hide the fact that we will be rotating the fruit so the cut lines up with the slicing action.

- ✓ The slice has to go past the centre of the fruit for it to count. This makes sense or the fruit wouldn't split into two.

- ✓ The gravity and "physics" in the game will be simple and faked so you don't have to worry about third party physics libraries or the complex maths involved in writing your own.

Flying gravity fruit

We are going to assume that the display size is 800 pixels wide by 600 pixels high, with the origin (coordinates 0,0) being in the top left corner.

Each item of fruit will be randomly placed off the bottom of the screen to begin with. It will move up the screen at a random speed, gradually decelerating until it starts falling back down again. When it falls off the bottom of the screen, a new piece of fruit will be generated and the process repeats.

The pseudo code might look like this:

```
Melon1X = 0
Melon1Y = 700
Melon2X = 0
Melon2Y = 700
Melon1AddY = 0
Melon2AddY = 0
Melon1Angle = 0
Melon2Angle = 0
MelonRadius = 64
```
①

```
Start Main Loop
  if (Melon1Y > 699) and (Melon2Y > 699) then
    // New piece of fruit set up
    Melon1X = Random number between 100 and 700
    Melon1Y = 600
    Melon1AddY = Random number between -10 and -20
    Melon1Angle = 0
    Melon2X = Melon1X
    Melon2Y = Melon1Y
    Melon2AddY = Melon1AddY
    Melon2Angle = 0
  end if
```
②

```
if (Melon1AddY < 20) then Melon1AddY=Melon1AddY + 0.3
if (Melon2AddY < 20) then Melon2AddY=Melon2AddY + 0.3  ⟩ 3
Melon1Y = Melon1Y + Melon1AddY  ⟩ 4
Melon2Y = Melon2Y + Melon2AddY
if (melon1angle is not equal to melon2angle)
   melon1angle = melon1angle - 1                        ⟩ 5
   melon2angle = melon2angle + 1
endif

Draw melon sprite 1 at Melon1X, Melon1Y  ⟩ 6
Draw melon sprite 2 at Melon2X, Melon2Y
Rotate melon sprite 1 to Melon1Angle  ⟩ 7
Rotate melon sprite 2 to Melon2Angle
Loop End
```

Sprites

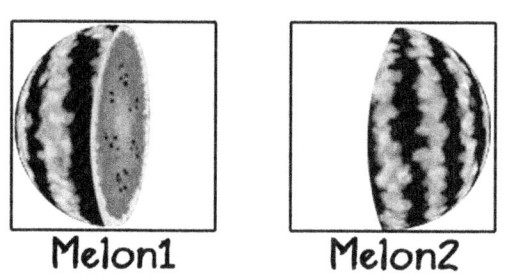

Melon1 **Melon2**

(1) The first part sets up our initial variables. Melon1X and Melon1Y tell us where on the screen the first half of the melon sprite currently is, and Melon2X and Melon2Y the other half.

We immediately set the melon sprite's Y positions at 700 so they are off the bottom of the screen. The Melon1AddY and Melon2AddY are variables we add to each half of our melon to make them move vertically on the screen. While the melon is whole they should both have the same value so they move together as if they are one item. The MelonRadius variable tells us that the melon sprite is 64 pixels from its centre to the outside edge (so the whole melon is 128 pixels across). We will need this later.

(2) Let's check if our melon sprite is way off the bottom of the screen using an 'if' statement. If the Y position of both halves is further down than 699 then we know it is off the screen and can reset it as if it is a new piece of fruit.

We set its X position to a random position across the screen between 100 and 700 to make sure it doesn't appear off the sides of the screen.

Then we set its Y value to 600 - just off the bottom of the screen.

We set a variable called Melon1AddY to a random number between -10 and -20. We will be adding this to our melon sprite's Y position to make it move up the screen initially.

This is a new piece of fruit so the melon's angle will be zero so it isn't rotated.

As the two parts of the melon need to stay together for now, we set the other half melon sprite to exactly the same values.

③ If the variable that we add to the Y position of the melon is less than 20, then we add 0.3 to it. This basically means that as long as MelonAddY is less than 20, we want to add to it to represent a gravitational force. A negative value for MelonAddY means it moves up the screen (and remember, it starts with a value between -10 and -20 so it goes up). A positive value for MelonAddY means it moves down the screen. We don't want it to move faster than 20 pixels per game loop so if it reaches 20, it won't get any bigger and the melon will have reached maximum velocity.

This is a very simple way of creating fake physics that make the melon pieces decelerate when going up, and then accelerate as they travel down.

④ We add the value of Melon1AddY to one of our melon sprite's Y position, and add Melon2AddY to the other.

⑤ If the angles of our two melon parts are not equal, then we rotate them in opposite directions by adding 1 to the angle of one part, and taking 1 from the angle of the other. While the melon pieces are together, their angles are the same so no rotation happens, but once sliced the two pieces need to look like they are being forced apart.

6 Draw the melon sprites at position Melon1X, Melon1Y and Melon2X, Melon2Y. Remember, our melon is actually made up of two pre-cut melon pieces which we draw overlapped to hide the cut when they are together. For some platforms you just need to draw Melon1 first (the background half) and then Melon2 second to make it appear on top. On other platforms you may need to specify a "z index" so the system knows which order to draw the sprites.

7 Rotate one melon sprite to Melon1Angle, and rotate the other melon sprite to Melon2Angle. Right now, our angle is 0 so they won't be rotating just yet.

This code will cause our melon to fly up the screen at a random speed and position, and then fall down off the bottom of the screen. Once it is no longer visible, a new melon appears and the process starts again.

Depending upon your screen size, programming language, frame rate and preferences you will probably need to adjust those numbers to make the game playable and enjoyable, but you have the beginnings of the game.

Slicing with a finger

Now we need to create our slicing code.

Let's add some more initial variables to our pseudo code before the main game loop.

```
SliceStartX = 0
SliceStartY = 0
SliceEndX = 0
SliceEndY = 0
```

These will represent the X and Y position of where our slice starts (i.e. where our finger first touches the screen) and where our slice ends (i.e. where our finger is dragged to and released from the screen).

Our pseudo code refers to a touch screen to capture those positions, but this could also be the mouse position depending upon the device you are using.

```
if (Touch screen is first pressed)
  SliceStartX = Get touch position X
  SliceStartY = Get touch position Y
  SliceEndX = SliceStartX
  SliceEndY = SliceStartY
end if

if (Touch screen is currently being pressed)
  SliceEndX = Get touch position X
  SliceEndY = Get touch position Y
  Draw line from SliceStartX, SliceStartY to
    SliceEndX, SliceEndY
end if
```

⑧

⑨

⑧ When the screen is first touched, it sets the SliceStartX and Y position to the location of the touch. It also sets the SliceEndX and Y position to the same location until we know where the finger slice is going to end.

⑨ If the screen is currently being touched, it sets the SliceEndX and Y position to the location where the current touch is.

While the screen is being touched we can also draw a line between the start and end points of the touch to show us where the slice is taking place.

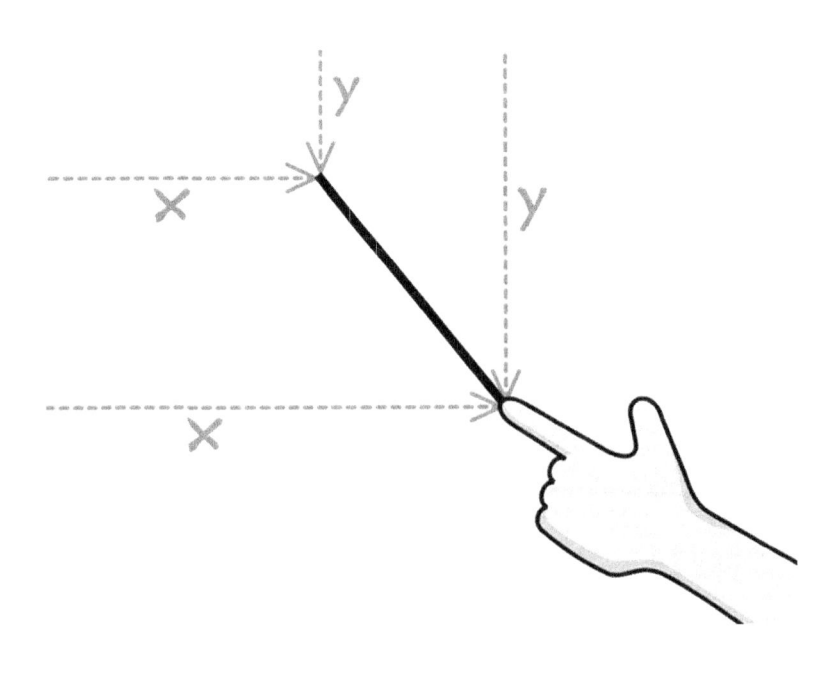

When we touch the screen the line starts. As we drag our finger around, it draws the line between the starting point and our finger. When we release our finger from the screen, the line stops. The line acts like an elastic band and stretches from the starting point to wherever your finger (or mouse pointer) is until you release.

This line doesn't do anything just yet, but it is important to show the player that their finger creates a visible "slice" on the screen.

Once you are happy that you understand how this works, move on to the next part to actually use the line and slice the fruit.

Slicing the fruit

We need to test if our finger slice actually comes into contact with the fruit. This requires some maths. Don't worry, I will go through it and provide the formulas that we need. We won't dive into it too deeply so if you want to know how the complex maths works, you can look that up later.

We have the X and Y coordinates of the start of our slicing line, and we have the X and Y coordinates of the end of our line. We also know the X and Y coordinates of our piece of fruit and its radius. This is all we need to find out if our slice line goes through our round piece of fruit. We need to calculate what is known as the Euclidean Distance of our slice line. This is basically the distance between the starting and ending points of the line so we use Pythagorean Theorem.

To do this we use this formula, just like in the earlier chapter:

```
SliceLength = SquareRoot ( ((SliceEndX-SliceStartX)*(SliceEndX-SlideStartX)) + ((SliceEndY-SlideStartY)*(SliceEndY-SliceStartY)) )
```

(This appears wrapped to fit on the page but it should all be on one line).

As we only need to check this maths while a slice is occurring, we can put the code inside the 'if' statement that checks if the screen is currently being touched (numbered 9 in the previous section).

Now we need a direction vector from the start of the slice line to the end of the slice line. This tells us the X and Y direction the line travels along.

```
DirectionX = (SliceEndX-SliceStartX) / SliceLength
DirectionY = (SliceEndY-SliceEndX) / SliceLength
```

By using that direction vector information we can find out how far along the line is the closest point to the centre of our fruit.

```
Closest = DirectionX*((MelonX+MelonRadius)-SliceStartX) + DirectionY*((MelonY+MelonRadius)-SliceStartY)
```

(Again, this should be all on one line). We add the radius of the melon to its X and Y position as we want to work with the centre and not the top left corner.

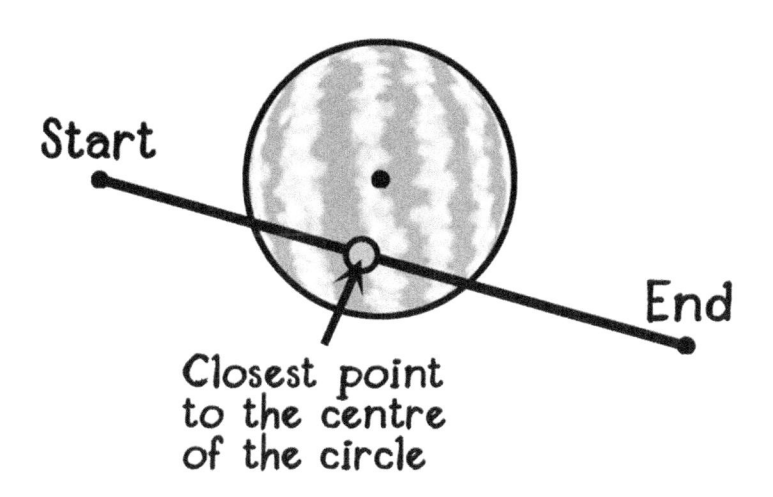

Closest point to the centre of the circle

Now we know how far along the line is closest to the fruits centre, we can convert that information into an X and Y coordinate:

```
ClosestX = (Closest*DirectionX) + SliceStartX
ClosestY = (Closest*DirectionY) + SliceStartY
```

We can use the same Euclidean Distance formula to find the distance in a straight line between the closest point on our slice line and the centre of the melon, and also to find out the distance from the start of our slice to the centre of the melon.

```
DistanceToLine = Square root ( ((ClosestX-
(MelonX+MelonRadius))*(ClosestX-(MelonX+MelonRadius))) +
((ClosestY-(MelonY+MelonRadius))*(ClosestY-
(MelonX+MelonRadius))) )

DistanceToMelon = Square root ( ((SliceStartX-
(MelonX+MelonRadius))*(SliceStartX-
(MelonX+MelonRadius))) + ((SliceStartY-
(MelonY+MelonRadius))*(SliceStartY-
(MelonX+MelonRadius))) )
```

All we need to do now is work out if the distance between our slice line and the melon is less than the radius of the melon, and if the length of our slice is longer than the distance between our slice start and the centre of the melon. If both of these are true then our slice passed through the melon. If it isn't then our slice missed it or didn't go far enough through it.

```
if (DistanceToLine < MelonRadius) and (SliceLength >
DistanceToMelon) then
  MelonAngle = ATan2(SliceEndY - SliceStartY, SliceEndX -
SliceStartX)
  Melon2AddY = Melon2AddY * 1.5
end if
```

The ATan2 function is a C++ maths Tangent function available in most languages that returns an angle between -180 and +180. We use this to determine the angle of the slice line. We then rotate our melon pieces so that the cut between the two sprites will be the same angle as our slice, giving the impression the slice has cut it in half.

We also increase the speed of one half of the melon by multiplying it by 1.5 so the two halves will separate and move at different speeds to each other, clearly showing it has been split into two.

In short, if our slice goes through the melon it immediately rotates the two pieces to match the angle of the slice. Because this happens instantly and because our fruit is round, the player doesn't really notice it. In the finished game it could always be hidden more by having sparkles or fruit juice come flying out. This is what all of these "fruit slice" games do which acts to hide the rotating sprites and also give the game some "pizzazz".

The two halves of the melon then rotate in opposite directions and move away from each other to show it has been sliced in two. The player would never know it was always two sprites.

It wouldn't take much to turn this into a full game. Add some more fruit flying around simultaneously. Add some items which should not be sliced. Add a score counter and perhaps a timer... and you're done.

Make your own maze generator

I am going to show you how to build dynamic, randomised levels for your games.

This is often called 'procedurally generated' maps which have some great benefits for your players. There is a slight difference, in that technically 'procedurally generated' maps use a 'seed' value so the same map can be generated again by simply using the same 'seed' value - but most have a random element and people refer to randomly generated maps using the same term.

It basically means that the levels (or maps) can be different every time they are played, automatically adding infinite variety and huge replay value to a game.

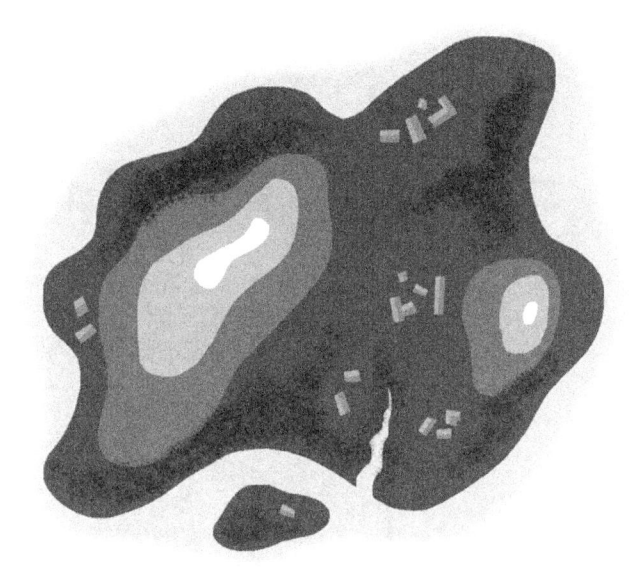

There have been some great games which use randomly or procedurally generated levels such as

- The "Worms" games from Team 17
- "Minecraft"
- Sid Meier's "Civilization 6"
- The "Spelunky" games
- "Bomberman"

Amazing mazes

Generating a maze is great for exploration or "dungeon crawler" games. You are making the player find their way to a point or an exit so your game has a puzzle element as well as any enemies or collectables you might want to add.

Remember:

Sometimes a maze isn't suitable for all games and would be too constricting for the player. Take, for example, a multiplayer shooting game. You probably don't want to restrict the players to narrow paths with only one way through. It would be much more playable to have more open spaces but provide lots of cover that players can dash between and hide behind. This is where an 'arena' approach is better than a maze. Hopefully you can take what you learn here as a base and build what you need.

As before, I will provide you with the pseudo code which you should be able to easily turn into working code for pretty much any language you prefer. You should also come away with the knowledge, the algorithm and the mechanics of how the systems work so you can expand them and use them in many types of game.

I will show you a way to create them quickly and efficiently.

A world of walls

For our maze level we will be creating our world using a grid of squares.

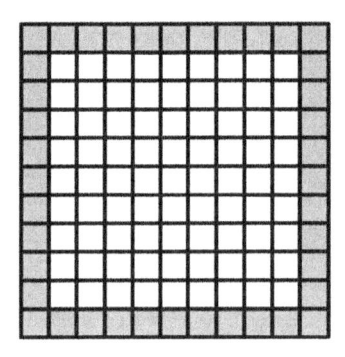

Each of those squares can be a solid block (a wall) or an open space where the player can move. Other people's routines create walls between squares but I find my way makes it easier to detect walls and spaces out pathways.

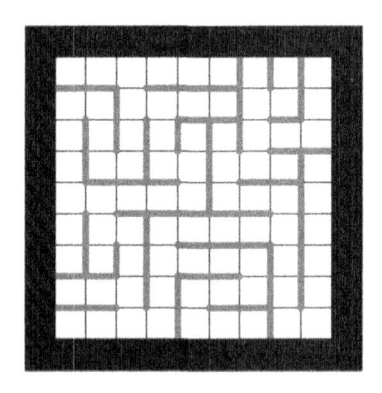

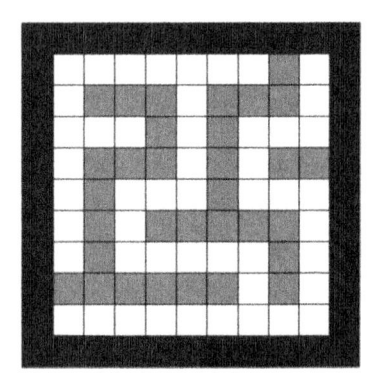

I will show you how to make this using a flat 2D level design but you could use the exact same system to build the levels in 3D, and even expand it to create multi-height maps over several floors.

We will automatically make all of the surrounding squares solid so the player cannot find themselves outside of the map.

Mazes are great for making the player work out where they need to go. No matter where you put the player to begin with, and where you put their final destination (whether that is an exit or to collect a key etc.), it must be solvable. You can't have any paths which are completely sealed off from the rest of the maze.

There are many different ways to generate mazes including Kruskal's algorithm, Prim's algorithm, Wilson's algorithm, and the Aldous-Broder algorithm, but probably the simplest is known as a "recursive backtracker" algorithm. That is what we will be using with a 'stack' to allow quite large mazes to be generated if needed. Don't worry if this sounds complicated as I will break things down and simplify it as much as possible. The only downside of this type of maze is that apart from being able to decide how big the maze is, you don't have control over how easy or difficult it is to solve. Sometimes you might have a very easy maze and sometimes a very difficult maze.

Apart from its simplicity to make, another benefit of this type of maze is that every other square going horizontally and vertically is guaranteed to be open. This makes randomly placing collectable items much easier without them appearing inside a wall. Not only that, but each corner will also always be accessible so you can place starting and ending points in any of those if you wish.

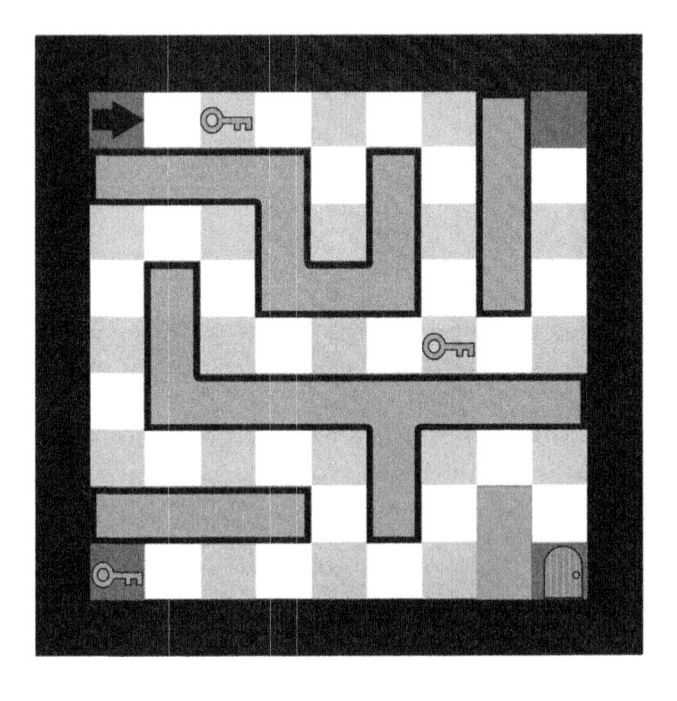

The theory

To make things easy, we will create an 11 by 11 brick maze. It needs to be an odd number of rows and columns to allow for an even number of paths.

We can create a two dimensional array to hold our maze, where each block has an X and a Y coordinate. If a block's value is 1, it is a wall. If it's a 0, it is open and the player can move into it.

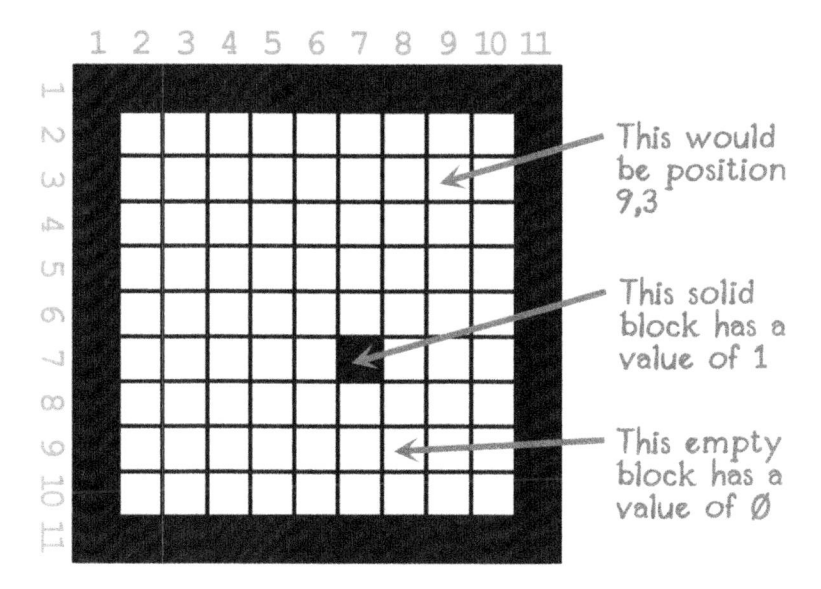

This would be position 9,3

This solid block has a value of 1

This empty block has a value of 0

We also need to create a 'stack', which will temporarily hold the coordinates of empty blocks so when we reach a dead end, we can 'backtrack' our way back up our path and make more paths in different directions. This is how this type of maze generation – the "recursive backtracker", gets its name.

The border blocks will all be solid to prevent the player from falling off the edge. We will also fill in all of the inner blocks for now so that we can carve our maze out of it. This would be the same as setting every position in our 2 dimensional maze array to a 1.

Let's start in the top left corner. This will be our current position.

We need to clear that block and add its location to our 'stack'. That square is 2,2 (or 2 across and 2 down).

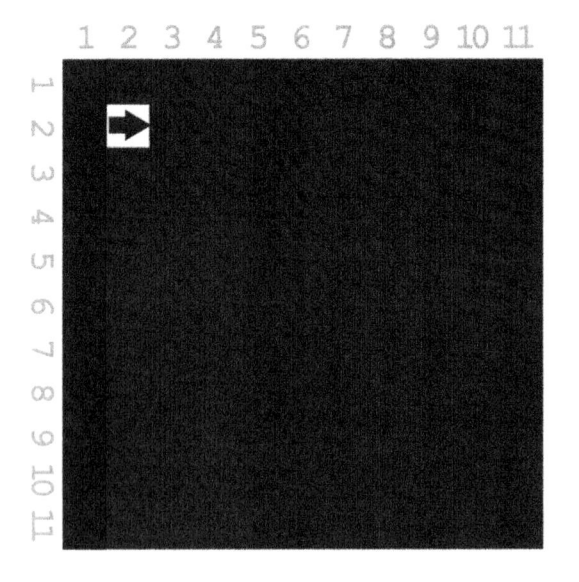

STACK
2,2

This is where we would start our loop in the code. If there are any locations left in our stack then we still need to carve out paths. If there are no locations left in our stack then we have finished building our maze and can quit the loop. We know there is something in the stack because we just added it, so we continue.

We need to check if there are any solid blocks two spaces away, in any of the four directions. As we are right next to two borders we don't need to check up or left.

We have solid blocks in two directions so we can randomly choose one and carve a path to it. Let's choose to go right.

We can now make the positions 3,2 and 4,2 in our maze array empty, i.e. they equal 0.

We can also move to our new position (4,2) and add that location to our stack.

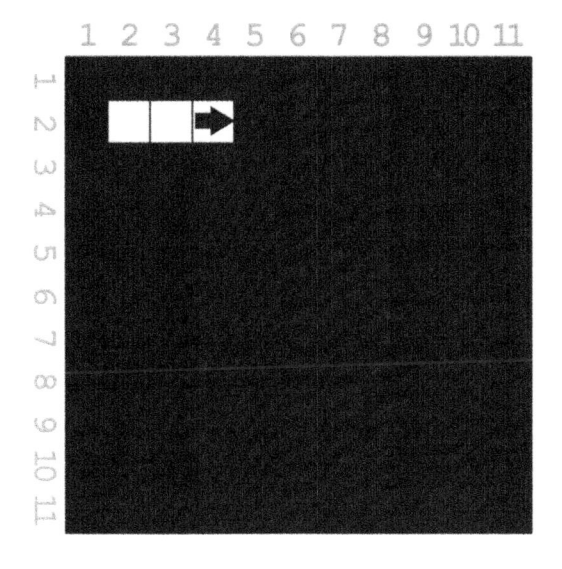

```
STACK
2,2
4,2
```

We loop through the process of looking for solid blocks 2 steps away in all directions.

There are three directions available but 1 (to the left) is already empty so we cannot choose that one. Randomly we pick another one of the other two, in this case let's say 4,4 (i.e. down).

We set 4,3 and 4,4 to be empty (a value of 0).

We move our current position into 4,4 and add that location to our stack.

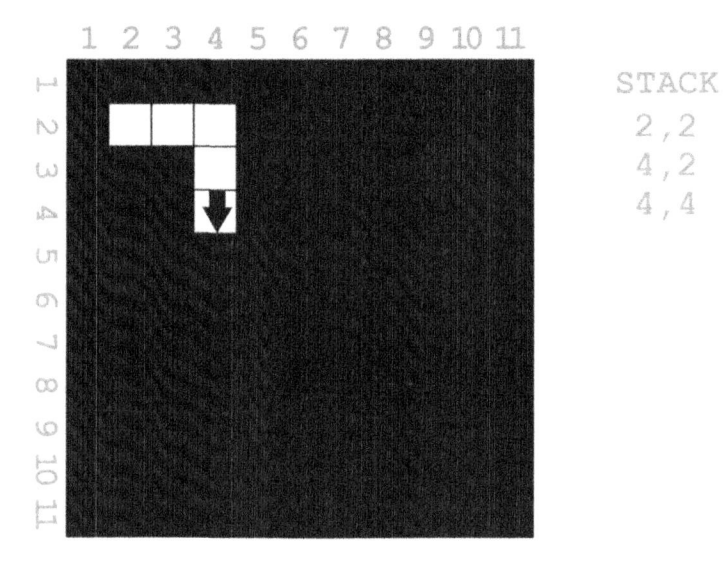

```
        1 2 3 4 5 6 7 8 9 10 11        STACK
     1                                   2,2
     2  ■ ■ ■                            4,2
     3      ■                            4,4
     4      ↓
     5
     6
     7
     8
     9
    10
    11
```

If we ever get to a square where there are no solid blocks available in any direction, then we remove it from the stack, and move our position to the last location left on the stack. This is the backtracking part.

You can go through the following pseudo code to see how you can make the program work in your own preferred programming language. It is commented (the lines starting with two slashes //) so you can see exactly what each part does.

Pseudo maze generation code

```
// Set up our 2 dimensional array to hold the maze blocks.
// Each block is stored as maze[x position, y position]
maze = array(11,11)

// Fill our maze with blocks, i.e. all spaces have a value of 1
for row=1 to 11
   for column=1 to 11
      maze[column,row] = 1
   next column
next row

// Set up our empty path stack
pathstack = array()

// Create an array to hold possible exits available
exits = array()

// Set our starting position
currentX = 2
currentY = 2

// Make our starting location an empty block in our array...
maze[currentX, currentY] = 0

// ...and add the location to our stack
add currentX,currentY to pathstack

Start Loop

  // Clear the exits array
  empty exits array

  // Check if there is a solid block to our left (and we aren't
  // next to the border)
  If currentX > 2 and maze[currentX-2, currentY] = 1 then add
"Left" to exits array

  // Check if there is a solid block to our right (and we aren't
  // next to the border)
  If currentX < 10 and maze[currentX+2, currentY] = 1 then add
"Right" to exits array
```

```
   // Check if there is a solid block above us (and we aren't
   // next to the border)
   If currentY > 2 and maze[currentX, currentY-2] = 1 then add
"Up" to exits array

   // Check if there is a solid block below us (and we aren't
   // next to the border)
   If currentY < 10 and maze[currentX, currentY+2] = 1 then add
"Down" to exits array

   // Check if there are no exits available
   if exits array is empty then
      delete last entry in pathstack
      set currentX and currentY to previous entry in pathstack
   else
      // There are exits available from our current location.
      // Pick a random exit from the exits array
      randExit = random number between 1 & total size exits array

      if exits[randExit] = "Left" then
         // Clear the block next to us on the left
         maze[currentX-1,currentY] = 0
         // Move 2 blocks to the left
         currentX = currentX - 2
      endif

      if exits[randExit] = "Right" then
         // Clear the block next to us on the right
         maze[currentX+1,currentY] = 0
         // Move 2 blocks to the right
         currentX = currentX + 2
      endif

      if exits[randExit] = "Up" then
         // Clear the block above us
         maze[currentX,currentY-1] = 0
         // Move 2 blocks up
         currentY = currentY - 2
      endif

      if exits[randExit] = "Down" then
         // Clear the block below us
         maze[currentX,currentY+1] = 0
         // Move 2 blocks down
         currentY = currentY + 2
      endif
```

```
    // Now clear our new current location in the maze
    maze[currentX,currentY] = 0

    // Add the current location to the stack
    add currentX,currentY to pathstack
  end if

Repeat loop until the pathstack is empty

// Maze is complete. Now draw it!
for row=1 to 11
  for column=1 to 11
    if maze[column,row] = 1 then draw block at column,row
  next column
next row
```

Important maze notes

The size of the maze can be much bigger than we have made here and will still be generated quickly. The only thing to bear in mind is that the bigger the maze, the more memory needed to hold the maze array and stack.

It can even be used to generate mazes in 3D. You can quickly see how this could be used in an above view game or in a 'first person' game where you run around the maze.

Be aware that whenever you generate random levels, maps or other designs - it is possible that it could inadvertently generate mazes which resemble letters, symbols, rude drawings or even swastikas. Having an above view game will emphasise this, whereas it might be less obvious if you make a first-person type game.

You don't have to include the random maze generator within your game to make use of it. Instead, you could use it in a level editor just to create levels which you then save or tweak to include in your game. You then have full control over how they look, how difficult the level may be to navigate, and where items are placed. You still get the benefit of having the levels initially generated to save you time. With larger mazes and maps, this could be a HUGE help.

Artificial Intelligence - A.I.

The terms "Artificial Intelligence" and "Machine Learning" are often used interchangeably. Strictly speaking, "Artificial Intelligence" is the general term for any computer system that emulates human thought processes. "Machine Learning" is the actual workings and rules behind the scenes that allow the system to learn and make decisions.

We could have a big discussion about whether being able to recall data or draw conclusions from it can be called real "intelligence" or whether that should require original thought, but that is such a big subject with arguments from both sides that we won't go into it here.

Machine Learning will always rely on data (or input) to learn from. There are two main uses for Machine Learning in general.

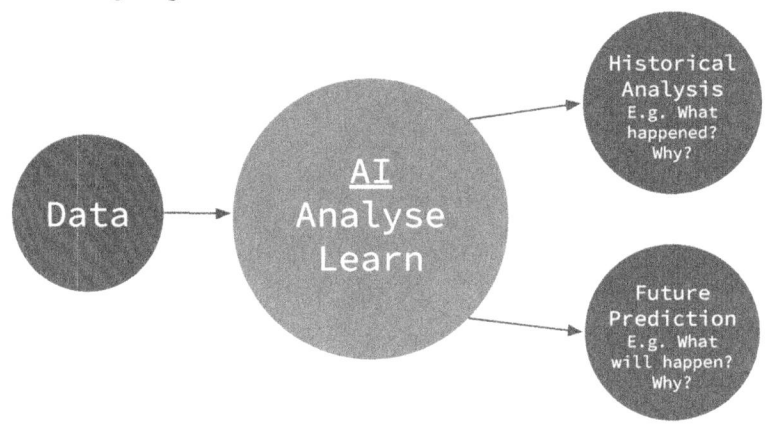

```
Data → AI Analyse Learn → Historical Analysis
                          E.g. What happened? Why?
                        → Future Prediction
                          E.g. What will happen? Why?
```

The AI part of the system will take the input data and analyse it to learn from it. This is also known as "training" the system. The more data it is given, the more it learns and the more accurate it can be. It will then use input data to compare with what it has learnt and try to understand it.

The first use for AI is to look at historical data and try to work out what happened, and why. In the real world this could be used to work out why certain disasters occurred, why events unfolded in a particular way or to recognise patterns.

The second use for AI is to take current data and try to predict what will happen in the future. A real world example might be to look at certain weather conditions and predict hurricanes appearing or droughts which haven't happened yet.

A.I. in a game, example 1

Machine Learning in gaming is becoming more and more important, allowing games to make better decisions based on users actions and to better emulate what real human players would do.

For example, take computer controlled soldiers in a game. If they can learn your strategies to flank and work as a team, it makes for a much more interesting and challenging game. Be aware that they might become too good so sometimes they may have to be "dumbed down" to make the game more enjoyable.

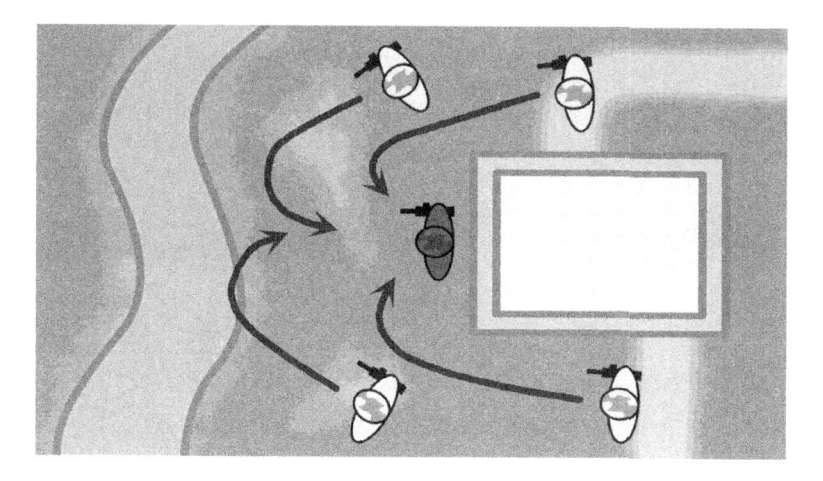

They could learn this behaviour by being taught about real events or by monitoring how human players work together. The longer they learn, the better their tactics would be.

A.I. in a game, example 2

Another example could be a car racing game with computer controlled vehicles. If those cars base their track positioning and speed when approaching corners on how real human players drive then it vastly improves the experience for the player and it doesn't feel like their opponents are running on rails.

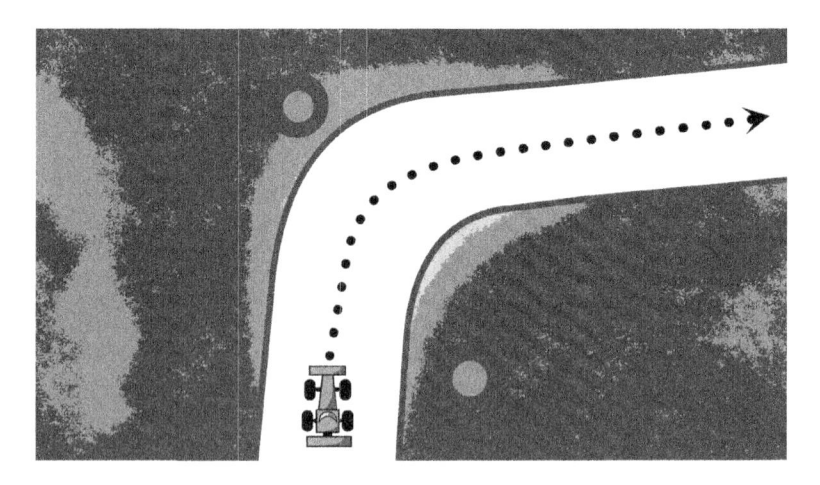

The above image is pretty much how an old-school racing game would work without AI. The computer controlled vehicle stays at a fixed speed and it tries to stay in a similar position centred on the track, all the way round. It doesn't look very realistic and is very easy to spot by real players. One of the aims of modern racing games is to make the player feel like they could be racing against other real people.

Now look at how a real racing driver might take the corner.

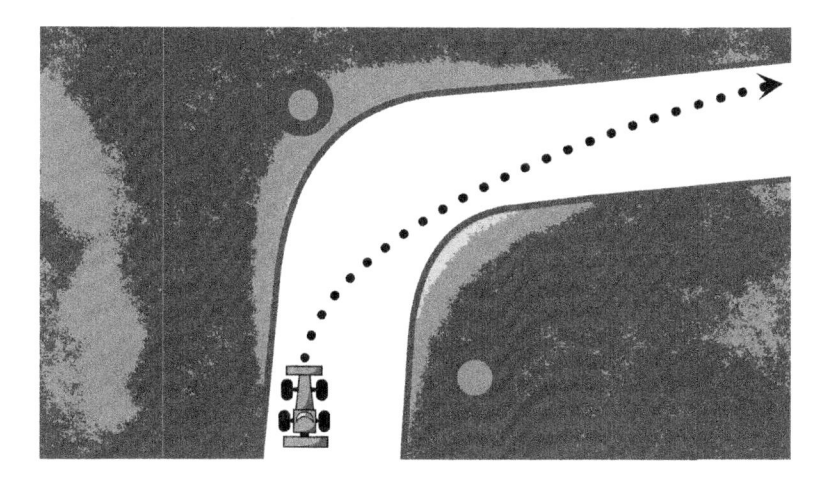

They position themselves wide and drop their speed as they approach the bend. Then accelerate through the turn towards the apex, leaving it closer to the outer edge to get the most speed with the most traction. It is basically creating a much bigger turning circle so the overall speed can be faster without losing grip and spinning out.

The game could be taught this by monitoring real races, observing good players, or by being left to try all different combinations of position and speed so it can learn the best results in the quickest time for each part of the track.

G.I.G.O.

There is an old acronym in computing - "G.I.G.O". It stands for "Garbage In, Garbage Out", and has never been more prevalent when talking about Machine Learning.

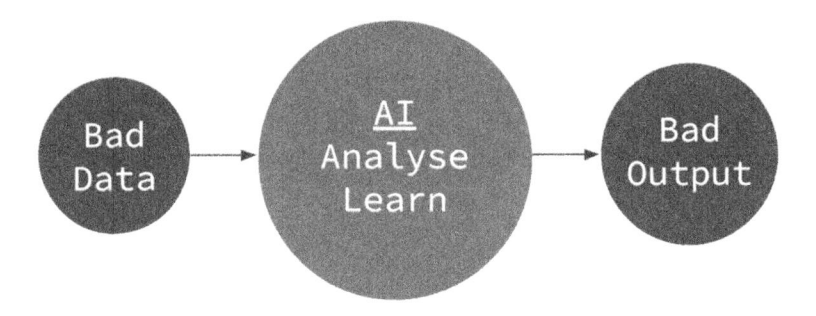

```
Bad Data → AI Analyse Learn → Bad Output
```

If the data you give the system to learn from is poor quality, incorrect, or just plain bad then it won't know any better, and what you get out of it will be wrong decisions, poor choices and bad output. If what it generates is useless then it isn't worth using.

A classic modern example of this was Microsoft's "Tay" chat bot. It was launched on Twitter and the world was allowed to interact with it, ask questions and make statements, all of which it would learn from to improve its interactions and behave more human.

Sadly, it was bombarded by trolls online who gave it false information and horrible prejudiced data. Due to the input data not being filtered or checked it learned from this and thought it was normal human behaviour so started to repeat these appalling statements.

This wasn't really Microsoft's fault as Tay did what it was set up to do - it learned from the input it was given, emulated it and made decisions and statements based on that. Unfortunately it was a case of garbage input leading to garbage output and is a clear lesson on checking or filtering what is fed into a system to ensure truth and quality.

A closed system would fix this where the input that is fed into it is closely controlled to begin with to ensure it is good. Once it has learned "enough" then the learning ability can be turned off and it can just analyse input and produce output. The "knowledge" it has gained is not tainted by any future input.

Making a brain - simplified

You can think of the nodes or decisions in a neural network as "Neurons" - just like those in a real brain.

The neurons are linked together with paths or "Synapses" - just like a real brain.

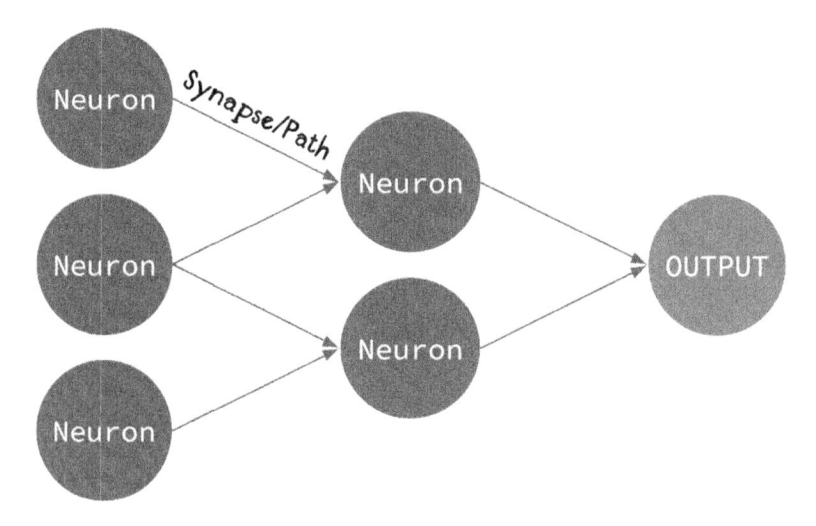

A neuron can be linked to any number of others using these synapses, and can be on or off. In technical terms a neuron which is "on" would be described as "firing".

Each synapse can be given a value or "weight". A neuron can be told to fire if the total weight of the active incoming synapses is above a certain value.

Don't worry if this sounds complex right now, hopefully the following example of a simple neural network will make it clearer.

Puppy Neural Net

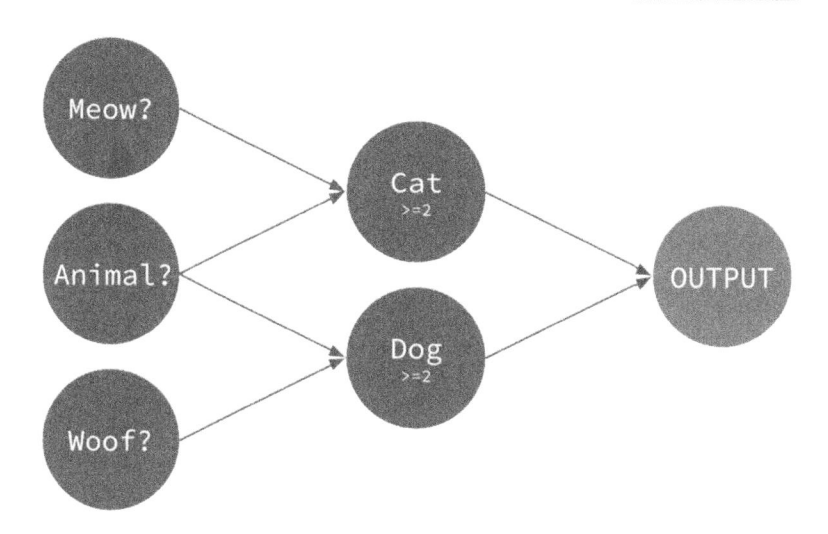

In this example, each synapse (or path) has a weight of one. In the real world, some synapses will have greater weights or importance than others, but we will keep things simple. The neurons in the middle will only fire if the total weights of all incoming firing synapses add up to 2 or more.

Let's start on the left. Our input is this puppy.

Don't worry - he won't come to any harm.

Each neuron makes a decision to fire or not based on that input.

Firstly, does it "meow"? No it doesn't so that neuron won't fire.

Secondly, is it an animal? Yes it is, so that neuron will fire and the two synapses leading from it will be lit up.

Thirdly, does it "woof"? Yes it does, so that neuron will fire and the synapse leading from it will light up.

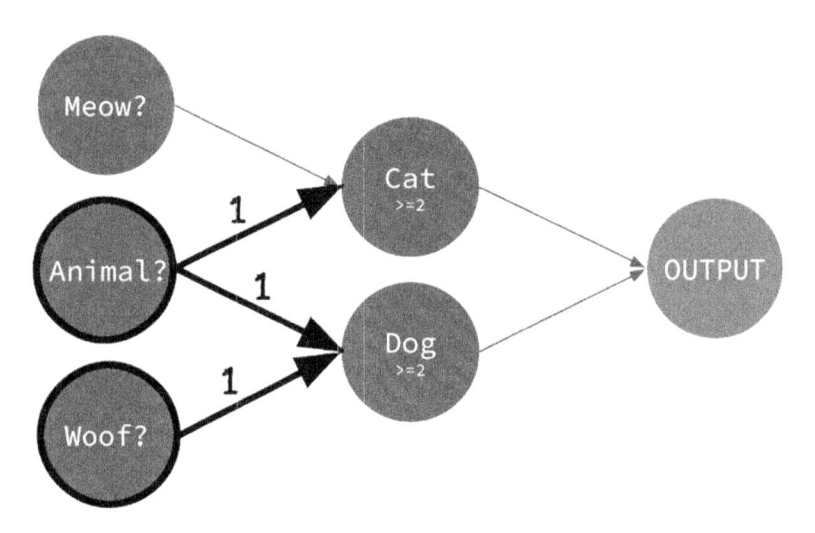

Now on to the second column of neurons/decisions. Remember, for these to fire the weight of the incoming firing synapses needs to add up to 2 or more.

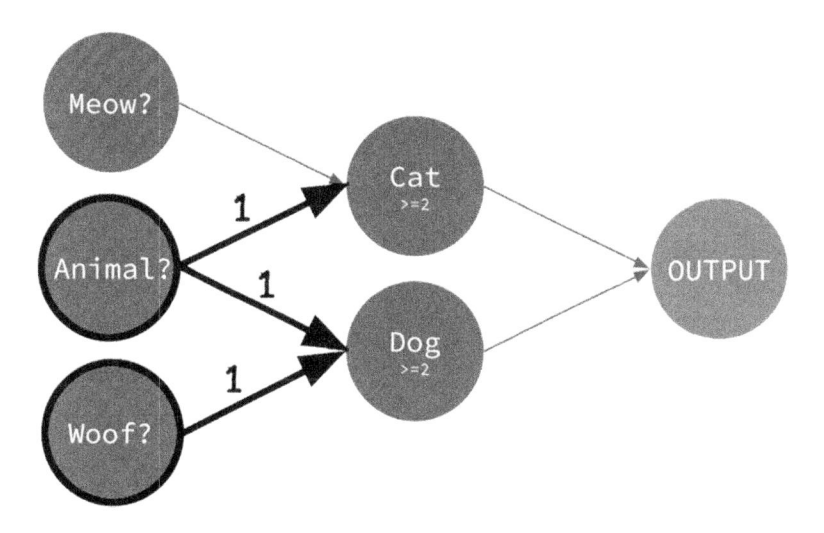

The top one only has one incoming firing synapse adding up to a weight of 1 so it will not fire. The system knows it isn't a cat.

The bottom neuron has two incoming firing synapses adding up to a weight of 2 so this one will fire. The system thinks it is a dog - which is correct.

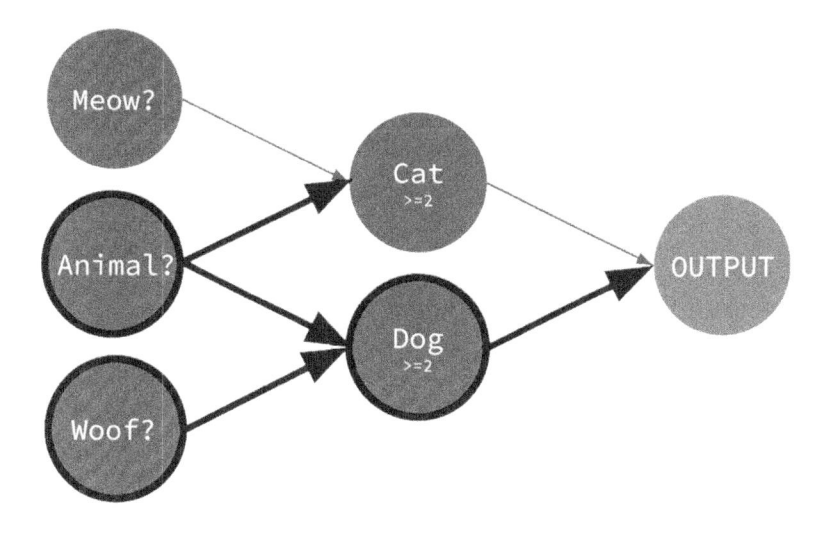

A working example - helping your player choose

There are a huge amount of other possible uses of a neural net in games. For example, you might have an open world and have it suggest the best routes to get to certain destinations.

Or based on what other players do you might want your game to suggest the next mission. Or in an RPG the system could learn from the player's actions and decide if an NPC (non-player-character) will help them or not based on how they treated them or spoke to them earlier.

In our real-world example I will show you how you could help your character choose an item from an in-game shop, making a suggestion based on what other players have previously chosen. It learns what other players have picked and predicts what the current player might want.

For our demonstration, this is a very small shop with only 5 items. The neural network is in learning mode right now so it won't make any suggestions or predictions. It is purely taking the input from players choices and creating the neural net.

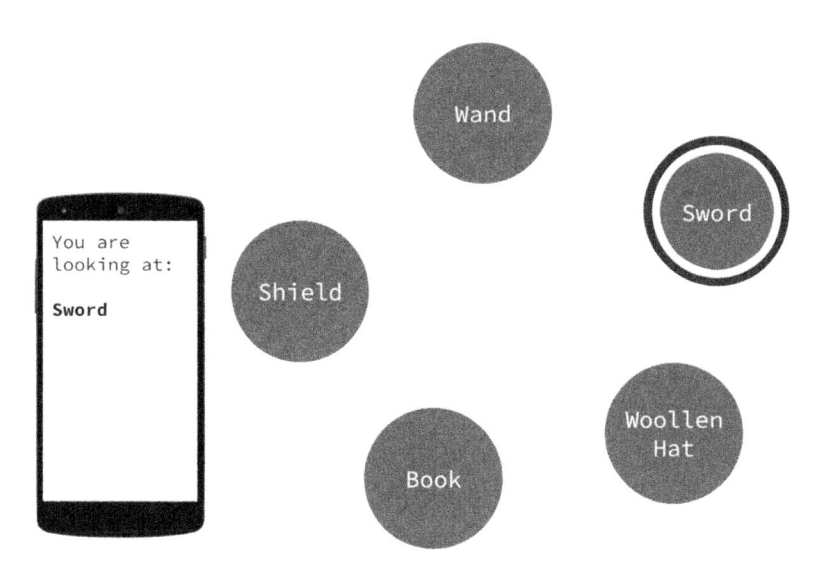

Player 1 accesses the shop and chooses the "sword". They have not made any other choices yet so there are no connections (or paths) to any other items. We just need to remember that so far Player 1 has chosen the "sword".

Now Player 1 chooses the "book". There is no existing connection between the two so we make one and give it a weight of 1.

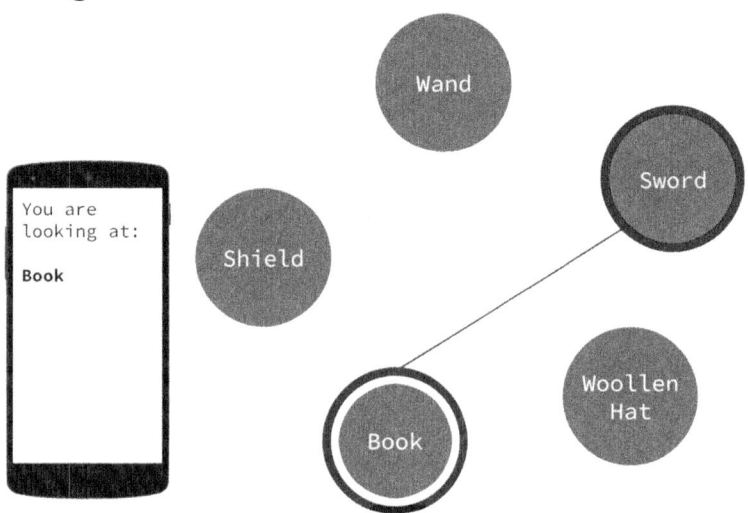

Now Player 1 chooses the "shield". There are no existing paths between the shield and the previous two items they chose ("sword" and "book") so it makes a path to both of those, with a weight of 1.

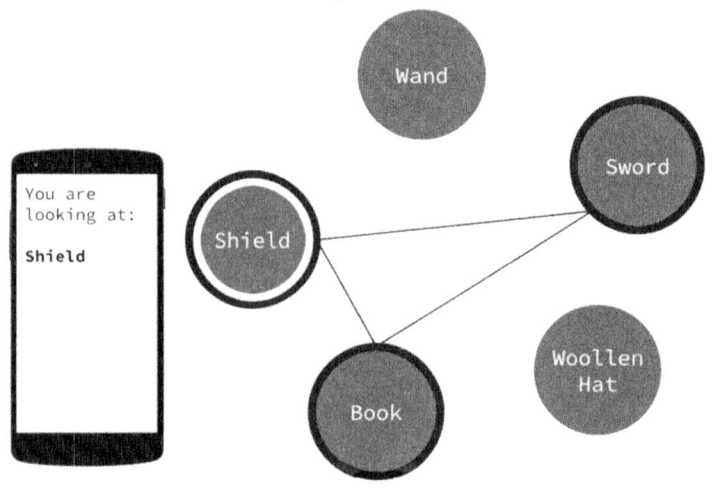

Now a new player - Player 2 comes along. We are still in learning mode right now. They choose the "wand" item.

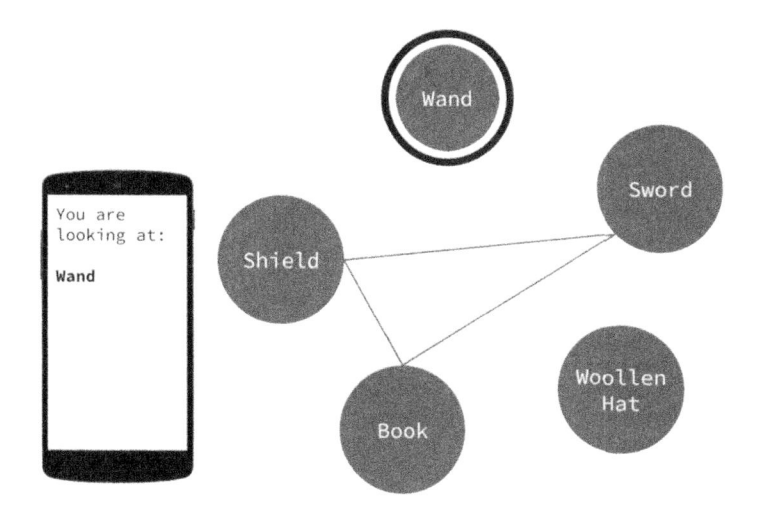

Player 2 then chooses the "shield". There is no path between "wand" and "shield" so the system links them with a path of weight 1.

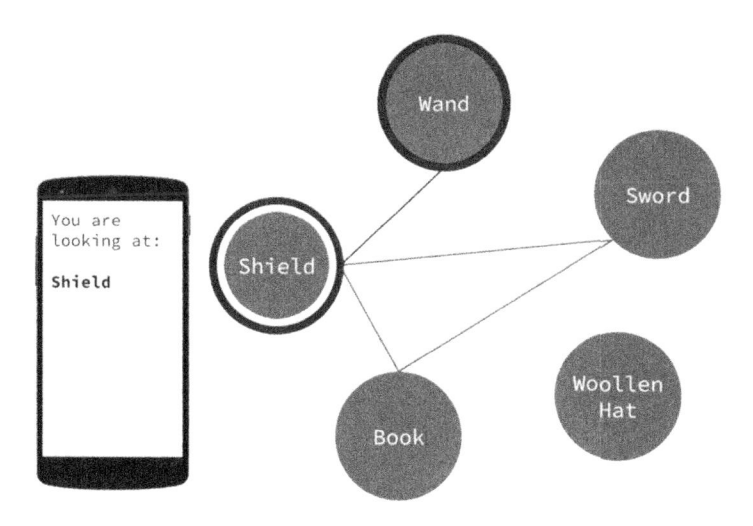

Player 2 now chooses the "sword". There is no path between the "wand" they picked and the "sword" so it makes a path with a weight of 1.

There IS already a path between the "sword" and the "shield" they chose so it adds weight to that path, making it weigh 2. It already looks like there is a link between "shield" and "sword".

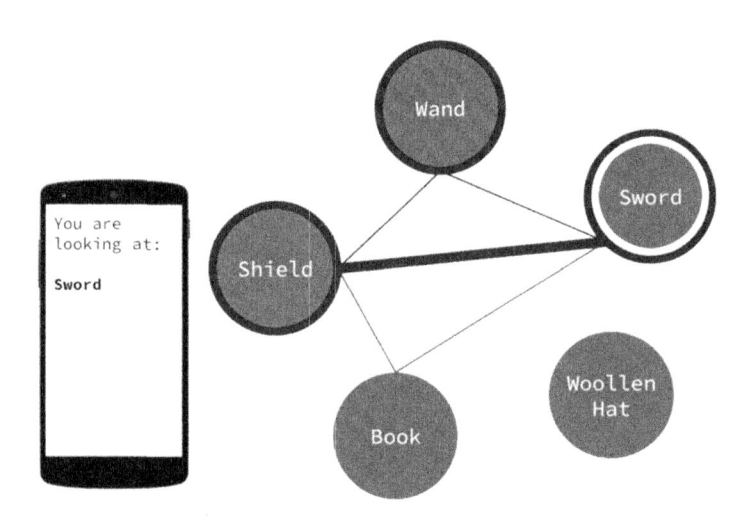

We decide that our neural network has been taught enough, so now we turn off its ability to learn, and turn on its ability to give predictions. Our neural network will be able to make suggestions for Player 3.

Player 3 chooses the "shield" item. There is a path from "shield" to "wand" but it is very weak - only weighing 1, so it won't be suggested. There is also a path from "shield" to "book", but again it only weighs 1 so it won't suggest that item.

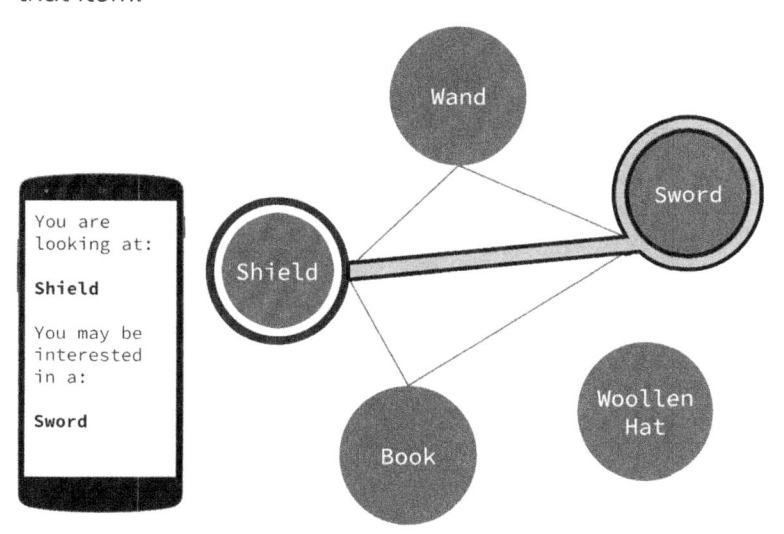

The path between "shield" and "sword" is heavier weighing 2, so it will suggest that the player may want to also purchase the "sword" as that is what other players have picked.

This is obviously a very, very simplified neural network and you would certainly want to teach it with a lot more players than just 2 before turning on predictions or suggestions, but hopefully you now get the idea of how you can make your own neural nets and maybe use them in your games.

A.I. is everywhere - but is that a good thing?

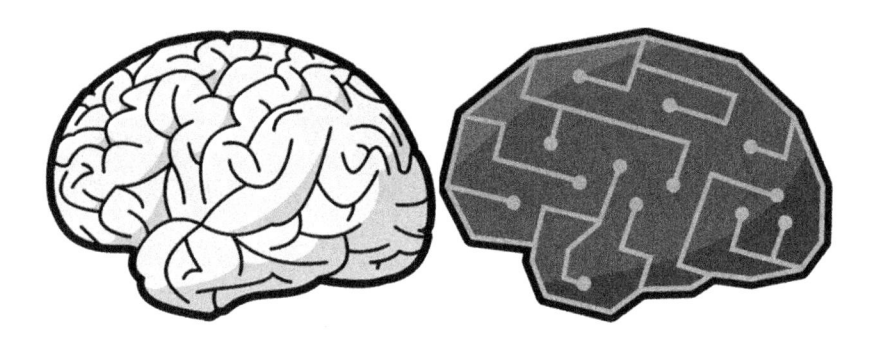

With the advent of "large language models" (LLMs), the term "artificial intelligence" is hitting all of the headlines again with the likes of OpenAI's ChatGPT and Google's Bard. There are strong advocates from both sides - those that think it is the greatest thing in the world to help people and improve productivity, and those that think it will be used against us and lead to the end of civilisation.

You need to make up your own mind, but my view is that it has the potential to be both. A.I. tools can be used just like any other tool. This can be for good or evil depending on who is yielding it and what they are using it for. Artificial Intelligence can and should be used to do the mundane or repetitive tasks which humans don't want to do and free up their time to spend on more important decisions and creativity. It's perfect for data analysis, recognising patterns and drawing conclusions or predicting outcomes, but it shouldn't be used to make automated important decisions - yet. It has not yet proved itself in life-or-death type scenarios.

It should not be used to replace creativity or as a shortcut so people are dissuaded from learning new skills or practicing to improve their abilities. This is a major problem right now where people see it as a way to get rich quick or produce things so they don't have to learn how.

A.I., machine learning and neural networks have been around for a long time and are used behind the scenes in places where most people don't realise. Artificial Neural Networks were devised in the 1940's so they aren't something new and those who appear against them probably don't realise they've been using them for years on the websites they visit, when they take photos on their smartphones, when they use a voice assistant, in video games, etc. The difference is that in recent times A.I. is being used differently and arguably wrongly. People are using it to "create" artwork, music, and yes - even code video games. I put "create" in quotes because the problem is that in my view it isn't really creating anything. These systems are trained using other people's work, mostly (at the moment) without their permission. Millions of pieces of artwork etc. are being sucked up by these systems that took artists decades of training, practising and honing their skills/talent to produce. The machine analyses all this content ready for a user to type a short sentence explaining what they want, and then it churns out amalgamations of this work with the user calling it a "new creation" and taking ownership of it - which in my opinion is not true and wrong. It is not using the original artwork for inspiration or creating homage to it. It is purely copying parts of it or the artist's style and merging it with parts from other artwork.

When used correctly, machine learning can help predict disasters, diagnose illnesses, find cures for disease, allow people to spend more time with family rather than doing repetitive tasks, and maybe even save the planet (or at the very least help improve it). But... it is a tool which needs to be respected and used wisely and appropriately.

Rant over :)

Whether you agree or disagree, hopefully this will make you think about the current uses of A.I. and where it might be heading in the future. Maybe even try some of the LLM systems out for yourself so you know what they can do.

You're not finished

The world of hobbyist game makers and independent developers is littered with unfinished games.

An unfinished game is no game at all. You cannot sell an unfinished game and you would struggle trying to approach a publisher unless you have a track record of successful titles under your belt. They need to know you can finish a game before they will invest in you.

If you did try to distribute or sell a partial game yourself online, it would be torn apart by reviewers and could seriously damage your brand.

You may be able to get investment using something like 'Kickstarter' if you can prove your concept will work but you will still need to demonstrate you can build the game before people hand over their money.

Be careful you don't rush the ending of your game in order to get it out. You can often tell when the writer of a movie or book couldn't come up with a proper ending or ran out of time and rushed it. The same applies to games. Be happy with its completion before distributing or selling it or your reputation could be at risk along with future projects.

> *"If you're not happy, your players won't be happy"*

There are many stories of early 8 bit games which had extremely tight deadlines resulting in them being released before they were finished. In some cases the games could never be completed by players as the ending was actually broken, such as the original release of "Jet Set Willy" with a bug known as the "Attic bug". Once the player entered "The Attic" room a graphical glitch would corrupt memory locations containing other rooms making some of them deadly upon entering.

Another famous story is that of "ET the Extra-Terrestrial" (the game based on the film) from Atari which is seen by a lot of people as the worst professional video game ever made. Its sole programmer Howard Scott Warshaw was also responsible for some of their best and biggest selling titles such as "Yar's Revenge" and "Raiders of the Lost Ark".

For "ET" he was only given 5 weeks back in 1982 to make it before the Christmas rush. Atari paid a reported $21 million for the game rights (equivalent to around $51 million in today's money). They also budgeted $5 million on an advertising campaign (equivalent to around $12 million now). The rushed game had players frustrated with strange behaviour like falling into hidden pits you could not get out of, and sales plummeted.

In the end, truckloads of unsold "ET" games were buried in the New Mexico desert and it was partly blamed (rightly or wrongly) for the video game crash of 1983.

Things are a little different now as most devices are connected to the internet so pushing out bug fixes and software updates can be done after release, but many players would argue that post-release bug fixes should not be needed.

A tip for you:

Don't be too disheartened if after months of development you decide your game just isn't fun.

This happens a lot and independent developers can spend years on various games before making one which they feel is worth building to completion.

Don't stick with a game purely because you consider you have invested too much time in it but know deep down it will not be played. Use it as a learning experience and move on. You may find you can use routines, resources and methods that you developed for the game on future projects to save time.

Test, test and test some more

Make sure your game is as bug free as possible.

Obviously it is impossible to ensure your game is 100% bug free as you cannot possibly test it on all platforms and in all situations, but never let a game be released if you know there is a bug. Get others to test your game too - as many people as possible. Friends are great for this (and usually won't cost anything!) but ensure they give you real feedback and don't just stroke your ego.

You have to be able to take constructive criticism when someone tells you your beautiful creation has more bugs in it than an episode of "I'm a celebrity - Get me out of here".

Using people with a range of abilities and gaming experience would be good too. It is easy to fall into a trap where you automatically think players will know how to control a character or where to go in a game. You may have put in hundreds of hours play testing it yourself and get blinkered by certain ways of doing things which are obvious to you but not to new-comers. If the objectives and controls do not become clear eventually you could end up with frustrated players who will give up.

Do you know where the term 'bug' came from?

In 1945, the first computer 'bug' was a real moth that flew into a relay causing it to fail. The term stuck.

Use the information you gather from play testers to decide whether to tweak your game or not. Sometimes you will get people say something is too difficult but they still worked out how to do it in the end. Don't dumb something down if you really feel that it would destroy the challenge.

While making your game it is often worth remembering that it is usually easier to make a game more difficult (e.g. add more obstacles) than it is to make it easier while still keeping it fun.

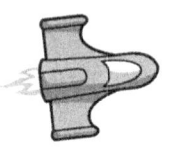

You may need to look into NDA's (non-disclosure agreements) to prevent your testers talking about your game before it is released. These are standard for the big game producers and with good reason. The time and effort involved in creating your masterpiece could be destroyed if a tester posts online about a bug which is fixed before official release, or gives away your surprise twist ending.

The 'unknown' factor

No matter how much people spend on development and budget for marketing, sometimes a game can become huge for no apparent reason. Something in it just 'clicks' with an audience and it spreads.

Social media can play a big part in this but getting heard over all the posts about other people's games (especially the triple "A" titles) can be hard. Equally so, you may have a fantastic and unique game but it never takes off for any number of reasons. Perhaps there is so much competition that people don't come across it. Or perhaps one person takes a dislike to it and reviews it badly. Maybe even the name of the game isn't enticing enough for people to try it.

Just for fun, which of the following do you think are names of real, released computer games?

- Zombies Ate My Neighbors
- Ninja Hamster
- Spanky's Quest
- Ninja Baseball Bat Man
- Tongue of the Fatman
- Rex Nebular and the Cosmic Bender
- Trevor McFur in the Crescent Galaxy

The answer: **ALL of them** are real names of real games!

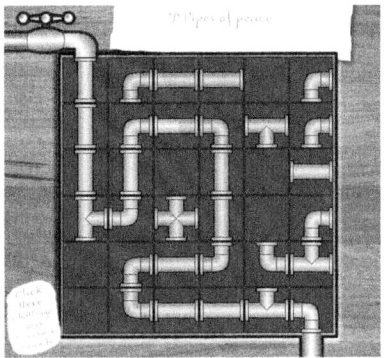

Some time ago I wrote a game called "Pipe Maniac" in Adobe Flash for the Facebook Games platform. It was a free puzzle game designed primarily to be a bit of fun but also help promote plumbing courses for a College and spread the name. It wasn't pushed particularly hard but had a few postings on Twitter and Facebook.

Suddenly it was getting over 60,000 unique players who were launching it over 100,000 times A MONTH! It was being played in 86 countries around the world.

It is an original game but I'm the first to admit it's not ground-breaking. There isn't a story, it is just a neat little puzzle game people can pick up and put down when they like. They can compete with friends to reach a higher level and post their scores on Facebook, but I wasn't expecting much replay value to be honest. Something made it go viral and I am still unsure as to what that was.

You probably don't want to hear this, but **luck** played a huge part.

A quick quiz

Try answering the following multiple-choice questions. Answers at the bottom of the page.

Question 1:
In computing, where did the term "bug" originally come from?

- A. A moth that flew into a relay causing it to fail.
- B. It's an acronym standing for Byte Unknown Glitch.
- C. A phrase used by early programmers for an annoying error, e.g. "this error is bugging me".

Question 2:
Why are Non-Disclosure Agreements (NDA's) sometimes used with testers of professional games?

- A. To prevent them releasing details of bugs which are fixed before launch.
- B. To prevent the leaking of surprises in the storyline.
- C. To control what information is released and when, for marketing purposes
- D. All of the above

Question 3:
To make a game popular and go viral, you need...

- A. Social media chatter.
- B. Good reviews.
- C. Luck.
- D. All of the above.

Answers:
1.A   2.D   3.D

Don't let reviews grind you down

I know it's easier said than done, but for anyone who makes games or apps, this is an important message.

As with any creative industry, if you make something popular enough for people to have an opinion about it, some of them will leave reviews. Given the choice, most members of the public will only leave a review if they have strong feelings about something. It's the "Marmite" scenario - either they love it or hate it and want other people to know. This is why you normally see a disproportionate number of 1 star and 5 star ratings with little in between.

There are, of course, exceptions to this if you pressure or reward people for leaving a review. In that case you will get a lot of "it's okay" - 2 or 3 star reviews which don't require much thought and aren't particularly helpful.

If you ask players too early to leave a review and they haven't had a chance to experience your game properly, you will also receive a lot of mediocre ratings and little feedback.

It's also sadly true that people are more likely to share a poor experience (in their opinion) than a good one.

Research shows that if you share an experience of something, psychologically it amplifies your feelings about it. So, if you share something that you liked - you are more likely to say that you LOVED it. Equally, if you didn't like something and share your thoughts - you are more likely to say that you didn't just dislike it, you HATED it.

Haters gonna hate

It is a fact of life that everyone's tastes are different. You will get bad reviews. You could make the most popular game in the world and some people will still dislike it because it wasn't what they expected. That's okay. It may feel like a punch-to-the-gut of all your hard work, and a knee-to-the-groin of the passion you poured into your project, but take a deep breath and remember...

You cannot please everyone.

Even the best movies had some poor reviews when they were first released. Here are some examples with the authors names removed to save them embarrassment, but they were all written by "professional" reviewers in professional publications.

Home Alone (1990) won 2 Oscars and 11 other awards.
"The plot is so implausible that it makes it hard for us to really care about the plight of the kid."

Lawrence of Arabia (1962) won 7 Oscars, 6 Golden Globes and 4 BAFTA's.
"Seldom has so little been said in so many words."

Gladiator (2000) won 5 Oscars, 2 Golden Globes, 5 BAFTA's, 37 other awards and had 104 nominations.
"It employs depression as a substitute for personality."

Jaws (1975) won 3 Oscars, a Golden Globe and a BAFTA along with 9 other awards.
"...not once do we feel particular sympathy for any of the shark's victims."

Inception (2010) won 4 Oscars and 152 other awards.
"...fall asleep while watching and dream up a better movie yourself."

The Sixth Sense (1999) was nominated for 6 Oscars and won 36 other awards.
"I just thought I was watching a bad movie."

Alien (1979) won an Oscar and 16 other awards.
"What is missing is wit, imagination and the vaguest hint of human feeling."

Star Wars: The Empire Strikes Back (1980) won an Oscar and 24 other awards, and is widely regarded as the best movie in the franchise.
"It's a big, expensive, time-consuming, essentially mechanical operation... about as personal as a Christmas card from a bank."

Why don't people like my game?

There will be some reviews that are deliberately incendiary.

It could just be trolls intent on disruption. For some, putting other people down (or the things that they like) is a way to make themselves feel better.

The internet is littered with articles that deliberately go against popular opinion to act as "clickbait" just to encourage interaction, increase views and perhaps even earn money from showing visitors adverts.

It might be someone who has just taken a dislike to your game, or another of your games, or your logo, or your choice in music, or your hairstyle… anything that makes them want to vent.

It could of course be jealousy. Everyone and their dog thinks they have great video game ideas and could do better than the experts - just like everyone thinks they are a web designer because they can use Microsoft Word or Wix.

I know it's a hard thing to think about, but you should also consider that actually, they might genuinely not like the game. It could be as simple as that. Most users/players don't think about all the hard work that goes into your creation. They just see that little thing they don't like. It might be the graphical style, the genre, a lack of triple "A" game polish (with a budget to match), the longevity, the fact it has adverts in it (even if it means your game doesn't cost them a penny), or something else.

But they're not even playing it right!

One infuriating habit of users is to not read the instructions. Then they'll give you a bad review and complain about it not working how they expect it to. *"Include better instructions"*, you might say, but often it won't help.

For example, I created a specialist app a while ago which used the gyroscopic and motion sensors in mobile devices to detect the tiniest amounts of movement and vibration to trigger an action. This was one of its many features but something users still have a problem with.

The first version of the app had a message asking the user to make sure their device was on a stable, flat surface before they began. That wasn't obvious enough for some reviewers, so I added the instructions at the top of the description on the app store pages with the heading "IMPORTANT".

It was still ignored by many. The next version of the app had a more blunt message saying "Do NOT shake or move your device" as soon as it started so there was NO WAY it could be missed, but to no avail. Even after making the message flash in different colours, I still get a plethora of reviews saying *"I shake the device and it goes haywire"*.

It sometimes makes me feel like tearing my hair out and screaming, *"Yes - of course it will! It's designed to detect the smallest of movements so shaking it will DEFINITELY trigger it. What were you expecting?"*

It's feels similar to them saying,

> *"I was running your app but when I smash my phone with a brick, it stops working.*
>
> *1 star"*
>
> ⭐

The bad can be good

Even if a review you receive is negative, you should still read it. The player might have some very valid points and enable you to improve your game. Or make a better game in the future.

Just reading reviews that praise you, and offer no constructive criticism, won't help you grow and learn. You might not like what they say, or agree with it, but everyone's opinion is valid - mostly.

One last word of advice... Don't be tempted to reply to reviews with anything unprofessional, even if they haven't read the instructions or have no valid reason for giving a poor score. Just accept it, and perhaps point them to information which might help them appreciate your masterpiece a little more.

Don't get angry. Don't get even. Just get on.

Recap

So, to recap some of the key points that we have covered in this book...

- ✓ Come up with a good idea for your game. It sounds obvious but it doesn't have to be a unique idea to become popular.

- ✓ Ask yourself the big questions to make sure your idea will work as a game.

- ✓ Learn a little about the psychology of your players. What do they want to play and just as importantly, what makes them keep playing?

- ✓ Be aware that you might have to think up new solutions to problems which work more efficiently on computers.

- ✓ Learn as much as you can about the hardware your game will be played with. This can help you make best use of the device and avoid its limitations.

- ✓ Maths is important. You might not need to remember lots of formulas but it will help if you know how to use them.

- ✓ Commit to finishing your game.
- ✓ Test your game and get others to test it too.
- ✓ You cannot plan for a game to go viral. Luck plays a part too.

One of the most important factors about making games is... **enjoy it**. If you don't have a passion for playing games as well as making games then don't do it.

Now go and make something great!

Printed in Great Britain
by Amazon